Three to Get Ready

Three to Get Ready

A Premarital Counseling Manual

Second Edition

Howard A. Eyrich

BAKER BOOK HOUSE
Grand Rapids, Michigan 49516

ISBN: 0-8010-3209-1

Scripture quotations not otherwise marked are taken from the King James Version. Other versions used include New American Standard Bible (NASB) and Berkeley version.

Printed in the United States of America

To
my wife, **Pamela Jayne**,
and my children,
Tamela Jayne and **David Kenneth**,

who deserve the thanks that only a family can earn. Their encouragement and patience saw me through the days of dark clouds which inevitably accompany such a project.

Since the original edition twelve years ago, my family has continued to be an encouragement to me and living evidence of the value of practicing the biblical principles of marriage and family living. Pamela has faithfully loved me through the undulations of life.

Contents

Foreword

From my perspective as the pastor of a large church and a nationwide television ministry, I want to contribute to the strengthening of the family and the proper establishing of Christian homes. One of the best tools for this task is premarital counseling. This is why I am pleased to write the foreword to this book.

The original edition of this work found an enthusiastic response among pastors in America and abroad. This revised and expanded version will be even more valuable. Previous users will welcome the new ideas.

Dr. Eyrich provides a sound model which the busy pastor can use in a step-by-step fashion. The innovative pastor can select components from the model to enhance his existing program of premarital counseling.

This is a book that should be found on the "most used shelf" of every pastor and counselor who is concerned to provide preventative counseling before couples embark on the voyage of marriage.

Dr. Eyrich is well qualified to write on this subject. His doctoral work in this area, his years of active premarital counseling in churches and counseling centers, his teaching of seminars to pastors, as well as his work with seminarians, equip him to write this practical and thoughtful handbook.

D. James Kennedy

Preface to First Edition

Early in my ministry I was thrust into the responsibility of officiating at weddings. The senior minister was incapacitated with
angina in the spring of the year. As Minister of Christian
Education, and the only other ordained member of the staff, it
became my responsibility to fulfill many of his duties. Although
seminary had prepared me for an exegetical, expository pulpit
ministry, it had inadequately equipped me for this important
practical function of ministering to those who desired to be married. My frantic search of seminary files produced one page of
notes which stressed the importance of premarital counseling
but gave little aid for its performance. The Christian bookstore
supplied no significant additional information. I humbly extend
my regrets to those couples whom I served so insufficiently.

These experiences in my early ministry prompted a determination to develop a practical manual for the pastor. This resolve
has been strengthened over the past eight years through a survey, personal interviews, and the research for my doctoral project. In all the literature—much more than when I was in dire
need eight years ago—there is nothing slanted directly to the
pastor which integrates theory and practice.

My hope in offering this manual is twofold. First, I desire that
the Lord Jesus Christ may receive greater glory through well-
adjusted marriages and Christ-oriented homes. Secondly, I am
concerned that more couples will experience the great joys that
God intends in marriage from the very beginning of their lives
together.

The design of this manual is logical and practical. In the
Introduction I offer a theology of premarital counseling. It is not
intended to be exhaustive. I shall be pleased if it challenges you

11

to a more in-depth program of premarital counseling and stimulates further discussion.

Chapter one provides a session-by-session and step-by-step program for premarital counseling. This section is intended to provide a guide-at-a-glance for each session. Once you have become familiar with the use of each component, this session-at-a-glance will provide a quick review of where you have been in the preceding session, the couple's homework since the preceding session, and where you are going in the next session. The regular use of this section (with your modifications built into it) will facilitate an inclusive premarital counseling program which will also be flexible enough to tailor to the individual needs of each couple. Chapter two is a discussion of some pertinent issues which relate to the process of premarital counseling as a whole. The third chapter offers some thoughts on the concept of an equal yoke.

Part Two is the meat for the skeleton of Part One. In each chapter the components of a counseling session are discussed. The tests utilized will be explained. What each component is designed to determine or provoke will be suggested. Once you digest the meat, the skeleton will usually be sufficient to guide you through the sessions. However, the meat is always there for a quick review.

You will find that I have used the terms *pastor*, *pastor-counselor*, and *counselor* interchangeably. This provides some variety where repetitious reference was necessary. On occasion, one or the other of the terms was specifically chosen to fit the context. These are readily noticeable.

I have tried to make this manual personal in style. From time to time I refer to my experience and address the reader as "you." However, a good portion is written in the third person because it seemed that the nature of the material demanded it. It is my prayer that you will find it readable, helpful, and convincing. I trust that this manual will motivate you to adapt (and/or adopt) this program to your individual needs and thoroughly counsel every couple who seeks your services as a minister of our Lord Jesus Christ.

Preface to Second Edition

It has been extremely gratifying to receive letters, phone calls, and personal thanks from many who have been assisted in the task of premarital counseling through the original publication of *Three to Get Ready.*

The intervening years have brought growth in knowledge and experience for me. In this edition I offer procedures to extend the usefulness of the original methodology in the practice of premarital counseling and in the development of local church programs that will benefit both pastor and couples. Pastors of larger churches should find the chapter on the class/group approach helpful.

I am pleased that my good friend and fellow laborer, Dr. Wilson Benton, allowed me to include his chapter. I also owe him a debt of gratitude for encouraging me to complete the work on this edition.

Acknowledgments

Many godly men have contributed to this work. Jim Longnecker, my spiritual father, set before me the example of a Christian husband and father. Dr. Grant Howard, my doctoral advisor, taught me, criticized me, and encouraged me. Dr. Jay Adams contributed training, guidance, inspiration, and friendship. Two other professors along the way also made significant impact on my thinking. They are Dr. Howard Hendricks and Prof. Robert Dunzweiler. Without these men and others, I would not be a man of God.

I also want to extend special appreciation to Western Conservative Baptist Seminary for an excellent Doctor of Ministry program and the privilege of publishing the result of my doctoral project.

Others who deserve mention are Mrs. Gayle Roper, Mrs. Delores Urey, and Mrs. Carol Babcock.

Acknowledgment is gratefully made to the many people whom I have counseled and the many students I have had. They have taught me much.

I also acknowledge indebtedness to the following publishers and/or authors for quotations from their works:

Psychological Publications, Inc., for the use of the "Taylor-Johnson Temperament Analysis" profiles.
The Broadman Minister's Manual, used by permission of Broadman Publishing Company, Nashville, Tennessee.
Design for Christian Marriage, by Dwight Hervey Small. Used by permission of Fleming H. Revell Co., Old

Tappan, New Jersey. Also *After You've Said I Do,* by the same author.

The Act of Marriage, by Tim and Beverly LaHaye, Zondervan Publishing Company, Grand Rapids, Michigan.

Your First Year of Marriage, by Tom McGinnis, Doubleday and Company, Garden City, New Jersey.

Introduction

A Theology of Premarital Counseling

Everything a Christian does should have a theological basis. Obviously, every practice of a pastor should be theologically defensible. Perhaps many pastors have been slow to develop a program of premarital counseling, either because they did not consider such a practice theologically sound or because they had not thought through the theological implications and, therefore, their responsibility. The design of this chapter is to provide a challenge to both of these possible reasons for the appalling lack of adequate premarital counseling.

Divine Institution of Marriage

We live in the age of the disposable. From the throw-away can we've "progressed" to the throw-away marriage. The pill, legalized abortion, and the age of "meaningful relationships" have invalidated the need for marriage, "respectable" sociologists claim. But marriage is not disposable in any age or society. It is the pastor's responsibility to see that people understand the importance of marriage and to underscore its God-determined durability in his preaching and by every other appropriate means.

Nothing lends more credence to the theology of premarital counseling than the fact that marriage is a divine institution, divinely delineated. It is a divine institution because God himself originated it (Gen. 2:22–23). He officiated at the first ceremony in the Garden of Eden. The establishment predates the fall, and God affirms it by his frequent blessing after the fall. Also, God directed its perpetuation. That the relationship of Adam and Eve was to be a pattern for man and woman henceforth is clearly expressed as the will of God by Moses in Genesis 2:24, where we read, "For this reason a man shall leave his father and his mother and cling to his wife and they shall become one flesh" (Berkeley). Note that "*a* man" shall leave "*his* . . . and shall cling to *his* wife . . . become *one* flesh."

Not only did God establish the pattern, he prescribed the ground rules. In Proverbs (2:17) and Malachi (2:14), God speaks of the marriage relationship as a covenant. In the Scriptures a covenant is a solemn agreement between a ruler and a subject. It is imposed by the former on the latter with appended blessings and cursings. It is evident that God views marriage as a relationship, the boundaries of which he has established and imposed on mankind. Therefore, when a man takes a wife and a woman takes a husband, they voluntarily commit themselves to each other and enter this covenant relationship before God with all its rights, privileges, and responsibilities.

God has delineated his reasons for marriage. The Garden of Eden was a perfectly suited abode for Adam (Gen. 2:8–15). He had unquestionable control and dominance over every living creature (2:19–20). He had a great responsibility to challenge his intellect and authority commensurate to it (2:15–16). Also, Adam had daily communion with God, unadulterated by sin. What more could Adam need or desire? In Genesis 2:18 God shares with the reader of his Word his divine answer to this question, and in 2:19–20 he shows the reader how he made Adam conscious of this need.

Two of God's reasons for instituting marriage are found in the succeeding verses of chapter two of Genesis. First, by bringing the animals before Adam, God made Adam conscious that there was no one like the Creator. Having grown up on an isolated farm, I can appreciate this scene more than the average person. The romping and playing of the animals must have created a great sense of loneliness in Adam as he became acutely aware of his uniqueness. There was no one to speak his language. There was no one with whom to exchange a smile when the squirrels played tag or when mother opossum came through the line with her babies neatly stacked on her back. In short, Adam had no companion—"It is not good for man to be alone." God's primary provision in marriage is companionship.

Secondly, in this same passage sexual intimacy is suggested by God as his purpose in marriage. Genesis 2:24 says that a man shall leave (sever primary relationship with) his parents and shall cleave (totally adhere to) his wife, and they shall become one flesh. "One flesh" refers to sexual union. It may refer to more, but its foremost idea is sexual union. A careful study of sexual intimacy in the Bible will clearly establish that God intended it to be confined to marriage, but free, frequent, and fascinating within marriage (1 Cor. 7:15). A word, *knowing*, which God has intermittently used to describe the sexual relationship beautifully depicts its intended intimate character. It is not possible to doubt that this intimacy is a righteous relationship when the writer of Hebrews declares the marriage bed to be undefiled (Heb. 13:4).

The third divine design for marriage is the procreation of godly children (Gen. 1:28). In the midst of their intimacy, a husband and wife are capable of creating new life—multiplying so as to fill the earth. Tim and Beverly LaHaye offer a comforting comment on Hebrews 13:4, which emphasizes this God-given privilege and responsibility. They write:

> . . . I discovered that the Holy Spirit's word for *bed* in Hebrews 13:4 was the Greek *koite* (pronounced koy'-tay), meaning "cohabitation by implanting the male sperm." *Koite* comes from the root word *keimai* meaning "to lie" and is akin to *koimao* which means "to cause to sleep." Although our word *coitus* has come from the Latin *coitio,* the Greek word *koite* has the same meaning and signifies the relationship a married couple experiences in the bed that they "cohabit." Based on this meaning of the word, Hebrews 13:4 could be translated, "Coitus in marriage is honorable in all and undefiled." Partners in coitus avail themselves of the possibility of the God-given privilege of creating a new life, another human being, as a result of the expression of their love.[1]

According to both testaments, God has clearly declared that marriage is to be permanent (Gen. 2:24–25; Matt. 19:1–15). He has instituted it. He has delineated its purposes or design. He has declared its permanence.

If marriage is instituted by God, should not the pastor, who in a real sense speaks for God in establishing this covenant between a man and a woman (I pronounce you man and wife) be extremely careful and reasonably certain that the couple whom he joins understands the nature and responsibility of marriage? Should he not be concerned that they are cognizant of the practical implications and demands of the state into which he thrusts them? Does not God hold him responsible for a covenant executed ignorantly? I believe an honest theological appraisal demands an affirmative answer to each of these questions.

Nature of Man and the Nature of Marriage

The Christian is the one who has had the power of sin broken in his life when he was united with Jesus Christ by faith (Rom. 6:1–10). However, he *is* a sinner saved by grace. Sin has not been eradicated from his being. All too often the Christian chooses not to enjoy the benefits of union with Christ and rather puts himself under the control of this deposed dictator, sin. Whenever this occurs he may become selfish, hateful, or resentful, and becomes capable of committing gross sin like adultery, murder, etc. In general, he becomes self-oriented.

Jane is a warm, affectionate, dynamic Christian woman. Usually she chooses to exercise her freedom from the bondage of sin in terms of her marriage. But periodically the complete responsibility of four small children, while her salesman husband travels three and four days a week, becomes the occasion for self-pity. This soon turns to resentment. By the time Paul comes home on Thursday or Friday evening, Jane has become totally self-oriented. Her words are sharp and resentful. She is unaffectionate and unresponsive as a sex partner.

Paul often has a tense week. Clients have been unhappy with delivery, planes have been off schedule, and the sexually provocative women have made it difficult for him to keep his mind pure. All of this presents him with opportunity to question why the Lord has given him such an abnormal existence.

Such situations represent the real world of the Christian. It is with this knowledge of who and what he or she is that the individual must enter marriage.

Marriage is an ongoing, intimate relationship. It is not one in which people can long hide who they are at any given time. It is not one in which selfishness is long tolerated. Marriage is the most demanding "I-thou" relationship which humans know. Everything that one partner is touches and influences the other. It is our supreme opportunity for companionship. But, as the Lord has queried, "Can two walk together except they be agreed?" This companionship demands unity. Unity requires the practice of love. Love is possible only as union with Christ is practiced (Rom. 6:11; 1 Cor. 13:4–8). Romantic emoting will soon be stifled by the responsibilities and temptations of life.

Premarital counseling can be effectively used to clarify to every young couple that human nature is not changed by a wedding ceremony. It presents an opportunity for the pastor-counselor to cultivate an appreciation for the nature of marriage and to teach the couple how to apply the solutions of God to the difficulties created by their own sinners-saved-by-grace natures.

You will find that this program is problem-solving oriented. It is an endeavor which will help people face realistically human nature and the nature of marriage. It is designed to raise problems (like those of Jane and Paul above) and to seek solutions from God's perspective.

Shepherding Responsibility

Sheep need a shepherd! The understanding of sheep in our modern culture is very limited. But when the Scriptures were written, the agrarian society to whom they were addressed grasped the impact when God spoke of his people as sheep and his ministers as shepherds. We moderns are able to learn much about sheep and shepherding, however, by simply observing the scriptural figures that God employs to describe himself and his servants.

In Isaiah 40:11 and Ezekiel 34:14–15, he speaks of his leading and caring. Through these prophets God says:

> He shall feed his flock like a shepherd; he shall gather the lambs with his arm, and carry them in his bosom, and shall gently lead those that are with young.
> I will feed them in a good pasture, and upon the high mountains of Israel shall their fold be; there shall they lie in a good fold, and in a fat pasture shall they feed upon the mountains of Israel. I will feed my flock, and I will cause them to lie down, saith the Lord God.

Every church-going child is familiar with the picture of Psalm 23, though he may not be cognizant of its implications in the historical context. In the New Testament the Lord Jesus Christ in John 10 speaks of himself as the "good shepherd" who "leads them out," who "goes before," and who even will "lay down his life for the sheep."

How the Lord's sheep need shepherding! They become "scattered" when there is no shepherding (Ezek. 34:5). Once the flock is scattered, the sheep become confused. They turn each one "his own way" and each "wanders off" (Isa. 47:15).

While God describes his relationship to his people as that of a shepherd, he employs the same figure with its implications to his ministers. Paul, addressing the Ephesian elders in Acts 20:28, says, "Take heed therefore unto yourselves, and to all the flock, over which the Holy Ghost hath made you overseers, to feed the church of God, which he hath purchased with his own blood." Later, writing in the Ephesian letter, he speaks of the pastor-teacher as one of the gifted individuals given to the church by the Holy Spirit for the equipping of the saints (Eph. 4:11–12). The word translated "pastors" is literally "shepherds." The infinitive form of this same word is used by Paul in Acts 20:28, where it is translated "to feed" with reference to the responsibility of the elders for the "church of God." Writing of this word, Bishop Trench comments, ". . . the whole office of the shepherd, the guiding, guarding, folding of the flock, as well as the finding of nourishment for it"[2] is in view. The pastor, then, as the Lord's undershepherd bears these responsibilities to the flock.

Does not such shepherding require the pastor to be involved in premarital counseling? Is this not a theological basis for his engaging the prospective couple in the exploration of the practical applications of the biblical principles which relate to marriage?

If the Chief Shepherd guides his sheep in "paths of righteousness," then as his servants we dare not do less. Just as he leads us toward a goal, (i.e., green grass and still waters in the picturesque language of Psalm 23), so premarital counseling aims at overcoming the tendency to wander by establishing goals and objectives and teaching couples how to attain them.

Stewardship of Lives and Wealth

In the nineteenth chapter of Luke, the Lord Jesus taught about stewardship in a parable. He spoke of a certain nobleman who gave an allotment of money to three of his servants while he was in a distant country. Upon this man's return, he called his servants before him to give an account of their stewardship in his absence and to reward them accordingly. Stewardship is an important theme in the New Testament, and it bears on a theology of premarital counseling.

From a pastor's viewpoint, it should be remembered that those people whom God places under his care are his responsibility. The pastor must be determined to invest his life wisely in theirs so as to realize the greatest possible return for his Lord. The pastor also bears responsibility for the extent to which they become good stewards of their lives (Heb. 13:17). If he discharges this responsibility to them and they still become unprofitable servants, they bear the responsibility, not the pastor. Premarital counseling provides the pastor with an excellent opportunity to act as a steward of God's children.

There will be few other times in any given couple's life when they will be as highly motivated to respond to guidance as when they are anticipating marriage. For example, when I was enlisting couples to participate in my doctoral project, one young man wrote, "Beth and I want our lives to count for the Lord Jesus and I believe that your program of premarital counseling can definitely help us." The pastor who capitalizes on this motivation will have opportunity to develop a stewardship which goes far beyond this initial contact. This encounter of seven to twelve hours can lay a foundation for the continual building of a productive life by the couple. Perhaps at no other time under any better circumstances will the pastor have the occasion to invest as directly in any particular couple. He will be able to assay attitudes, spiritual development, and the biblical knowledge of these individuals. Being in command, he can direct the course of the sessions to enhance their potential for a creative Christian life. This very personal interchange also places the counselor in a unique position for an enduring ministry.

Another matter on which the theology of premarital counseling impinges is the use and administration of wealth. The average middle-class couple in America will jointly earn approximately $900,000 in their lifetime. How will they use this wealth? Will a large portion be expended for needless medical and psychiatric assistance as a result of improperly relating to each other? Will it be administered with the proper spiritual priorities as guidelines? The pastor's guidance may well be the determining factor. Cannot he, at least to some extent, effectively fulfill his duty through a good premarital counseling program?

Redeeming the Time

The injunction of Ephesians 5:16, "Redeeming the time, because the days are evil," though having its contextual force—which is compatible with the arguments for premarital counseling—is here used theologically. The pastor-counselor always has more demands on his time than he can possibly fulfill. Therefore, premarital counseling should be a high priority to help him in redeeming the time. A pastor friend said to me, "I pastor a church of 500 and am the only staff member. I don't have time for premarital counseling." He does, if his priorities are ordered. A well-devised program would in most cases not have cost him more than seven hours. In another conversation, this same friend was bemoaning the numerous hours he spends in remedial counseling. A number of the cases which he mentioned involved couples and their families. I wondered how many of these cases were the product of his tenure as pastor and could have been prevented by thorough premarital counseling. My personal experience in marital counseling has convinced me that the average pastor could add untold hours to his future ministry through a proper program of such counseling.

Another aspect of this concept is the shepherd's responsibility to guide the prospective partners of his flock so that they too may redeem the time. Poor marital adjustment results in an undetermined amount of time lost in terms of the service of Jesus Christ. The case of Joe and Ruth is a good example.

Joe and Ruth came to the counseling center after three years of marriage. Their relationship had been deteriorating ever since Joe had pressed Ruth into an early marriage. They were both Christians when they married. However, they had a poor concept of the Christian life and a Christian marriage in particular.

When they came into the counseling office, Ruth was vocal and distraught. Joe was sullen and quiet. They both worked. Ruth was employed as a secretary, and Joe was retained by a law-enforcement agency. He worked odd shifts. To avoid the situation at home, he had also taken a part-time job which allowed him to work almost any hours he desired. This effectively kept them separated under one roof.

Though Christians, this couple had never become active in a local assembly. When they came for counseling at Ruth's insistence, their church attendance was infrequent at best. Subsequent counseling revealed virtually no understanding of God's design of the local church or the institution of marriage.

After the second session, Joe dropped out, vowing never to return to counseling. Ruth returned to report that she had left him and "gone home to mother." During this hour she was convinced of her responsibility before God to return to her husband. She said, "OK! If that's what God says I must do, I'll do it. But I don't like it." Ruth was taught how to begin to function as a Christian wife irrespective of Joe's response. Four sessions later (eight weeks) Joe resumed counseling, reporting that the changes in his wife had convinced him that all was not lost.

Six weeks later the counselor inquired, "Joe, what else would you like me to do for you?" He replied, "You can teach me more about what it means to live a Christian life." Is it not possible that this couple could have been spared three years of agony through proper preparation for marriage? Is it not possible that this could have prevented the loss of their involvement in the service of Christ? Would this not have been "redeeming the time" for both the pastor and people in this evil day?

This discussion of a theology of premarital counseling is calculated to do two things: (1) to demonstrate the theological responsibility of the pastor for premarital counseling, and (2) to encourage further thought, exposition, and writing concerning this pastoral obligation in a theological fashion.

PART
ONE

Preparation for
Premarital Counseling

1

Overview of a Program for Premarital Counseling

In the research project I conducted, three logical approaches to premarital counseling were compared.[1] The approach which proved most effective appears in this section in a somewhat revised form.

The degree to which the average local pastor will be able to utilize this step-by-step program systematically will depend on two factors. First, the needs of the particular couple may require one or more sessions to help them in the application of problem-solving techniques to a given situation. For example, the couple may be experiencing difficulties with one or the other's parents. The pastor-counselor should probe this problem, determine its dimensions, discuss its ramifications, and perhaps assign the couple to work on the problem at a conference table.[2] What better way to teach biblical problem solving?

Secondly, his facility will depend on the frequency and consistency with which he applies the program. To a large extent, premarital counseling is a seasonal task. Hence, every pastor can enhance the service he provides by having an established method as a guide in premarital counseling. The more he uses this plan, the more workable it will become.

This manual is intended as such a guide. It is expected that the pastor will modify it to conform to his own conceptions. But he will modify *the program* so that it becomes *his program*, which he can work effectively.

Each session is designed with approximately a ninety-minute time block in mind. The exception is the introductory session, which may be modified considerably. Some variations of this session may be as follows: (1) If two or more couples have requested premarital counseling,[3] the counselor may schedule separate half-hour appointments to qualify each couple and explain the program. He can then schedule a testing period acceptable to all involved and administer the T-JTA (Taylor-Johnson Temperament Analysis) and SAI (Sex Awareness Inventory) to the group.[4] (2) If he has not been qualified to use the T-JTA or if he does not choose to use it, the first session will be shorter than the program schedule. Of course, this will of necessity modify the second session.

As the program which follows is perused, it should be remembered that a detailed discussion of each component appears in Part Two.

Session 1

1. Introductory remarks
2. Determine the eligibility of the couple
3. Administer the T-JTA (Taylor-Johnson Temperament Analysis) or Trait Factor Inventory
4. Administer the SAI (Sex Awareness Inventory)
5. Homework assignments
    a. Do the Marriage Attitude Indicator (A)
    b. Do the Reasons for Choosing My Mate Inventory
    c. Study and discuss together: God-Designed Marriage
    d. Devise and begin program of family worship

Session 2

1. Interpret the T-JTA or Trait Factor Inventory
2. Discuss: God-Designed Marriage
3. Homework assignments
    a. Complete the remainder of the Marriage Attitude Indicator (B)
    b. Do the Comparison of Role Concepts Inventory and compare answers; discuss differences
    c. Read chapter three in Adams' *Christian Living in the Home* and do the worksheet on problem solving
    d. Write a paragraph on how 1 Corinthians 13:4–8 applies to daily living as a couple (spell out practical implications)

Session 3

1. Discuss communication
2. Discuss Comparison of Role Concepts Inventory
3. Discuss the character of love and other assignments
4. Homework assignments
   a. List any problems you have had with prospective in-laws
   b. Work out a proposed budget
   c. Discuss children, including: (1) number, (2) approach to discipline, (3) attitude in relation to house and things

Session 4

1. Discuss budget and approach to money (credit and borrowing)
2. Discuss insurance and investments
3. Discuss children
4. Discuss SAI
5. Homework assignments
   a. Listen to Dr. Wheat's tape and complete worksheet (*Sex Problems and Sex Techniques in Marriage*)
   b. Have a physical examination
   c. Discuss birth control
   d. Fill out Family and Social Background Questionnaire

Session 5

1. Discuss sex
2. Discuss birth control
3. Discuss family and social concerns
4. Homework assignments
   a. Discuss date of marriage between selves and families; list any problems or objections by families
   b. Discuss ceremony and reception
   c. Listen to Howard Hendricks' tapes (*The Christian Home*)
5. Selecting Family Traits

Session 6

1. Discuss family worship
2. Discuss the ceremony and date
3. Discuss the reception (ask for any forms you have requested they fill out)
4. Homework assignments

    a. List anything that has not been discussed to your satisfaction

    b. List any additional matters you desire to discuss

    c. Anything which pastor determines is important from his agenda

Session 7

1. Discuss agenda items
2. Discuss the couple's lists
3. Determine day for postmarital session
4. Close the counseling with each participating in prayer

2

The Pastor-Counselor and Premarital Counseling

The Pastor-Counselor and "Secular" Material

Some people will read this manual and ask, "What is a pastor doing discussing life insurance, budgeting, or sex?" The answer is simple. He is responsible for the spiritual welfare of his flock. To the Christian all things are sacred—even life insurance, budgeting, and sex! In premarital counseling the pastor can take the initiative to discuss a wide range of topics with the couple. Without this stimulation they may never have sought guidance in a number of these vital areas or even discussed them between themselves. Hopefully he can lay a groundwork for others more competent than himself to be of assistance in areas such as insurance and investments.

The pastor's main concern is attitude; but attitude cannot be determined or discussed abstractly. Attitude can best be observed in relation to the daily task of living. In addition, the pastor is interested in surveying behavioral patterns. Sinful behavior patterns can quickly stifle communication. Thirdly, lack of basic knowledge in any of the vital areas of life studied

in this program concerns the alert pastor, since this will negatively affect the couple's ability to serve Jesus Christ effectively.
Life is the legitimate domain of the spiritual counselor.

The Pastor-Counselor and His Preparation

Some basic assumptions

This manual is predicated on at least three assumptions. First,
I am assuming a basic Bible knowledge by those who would be
interested in using this program. Therefore, the content is not
encumbered with Bible references and argumentation.

Secondly, a knowledge of biblical problem solving (practical
application of Bible doctrine to everyday problems of life) is
taken for granted in most instances. If a minister or other counselor has not at least mastered the theory of biblical problem
solving (being a sinner, he may not always apply it), he can have
little success attempting to help others.

The third assumption concerns the art of counseling. Since
every pastor is called on for counseling, I am assuming a basic
knowledge on the part of the reader.[1]

Thorough familiarization with the program and its content

Before using the program outlines in this manual, the reader
should do four things:

1. Read the entire manual.
2. Do all the homework assignments which I have suggested
   the counselor complete.
3. Purchase or have the church library acquire the books
   recommended in the footnotes as possible further reading for the counselor or the counselees.[2]
4. A good exercise is to ask your mate to go through the sessions and homework with you. Discuss how you have
   handled many of these areas and how such a program
   could have benefited you in the process of marital
   adjustment.

The Pastor-Counselor and His Objectives

There are three goals in this premarital counseling program.
Each is important and worthy of the counselor's effort.

Obviously, the first goal concerns the counseling directly.
Premarital counseling should focus on establishing a thoroughly
Christian home that glorifies God and produces maximum enjoy-

ment for the couple. The counselor's activity in the program presented in the manual consists, to a great extent, of instruction and guidance. Frequently the counselor will give advice. Although some will disagree, I am convinced that young people desire concrete suggestions from a positive, competent counselor. They want a realistic set of guidelines which will enable them to develop a stable life together. Though they may not articulate it fully or comprehend it, their goal when they enter premarital counseling is very similar to the pastor's. If he can help them grasp this, his job will become considerably easier.

A second goal, which may be surprising to some, is to encourage church membership. In our day, church membership is neither important nor respected in much of the evangelical community; in some quarters church membership is actually discouraged. Many young people graduate from Christian colleges having never been under the care and discipline of a local church. Premarital counseling presents an opportunity to funnel these young people into the life of the church. It may be important to instruct them regarding this important aspect of the Christian life. One couple, for example, in my practice had been converted through a campus ministry on a secular campus. They had infrequently attended a local church during their college years and did not understand the need and value of church membership. Weaving this instruction into the program of premarital counseling emphasizes the close relationship of the church and the family.

Evangelism can be cited as the third goal of premarital counseling. Adams has concisely and correctly stated the case. When a couple does not qualify for marriage because of unbelief, he recommends, "Whenever there is reason to do so, he [pastor] holds forth realistic hope. ('Let's meet several times and discuss the gospel.') That is to say, the unsaved persons (or person) may be evangelized."[3]

The Pastor-Counselor and His Procedure

Advertising

If the value and necessity of premarital counseling can be established theologically, then every pastor is responsible to have a program. But merely having a program is not sufficient. He must create an atmosphere of expectancy. This can develop naturally over a period of time. Couples who have profited from such counseling will cultivate the desire in others to go through the program. Initially and occasionally, however, the pastor will need to advertise in the church paper, use sermon illustrations and other biblical, creative methods to encourage couples to seek premarital counseling. Though I firmly believe that such counseling should be a prerequisite to qualify the couple for marriage, it seems unwise to use this as a public inducement to participate. This is more appropriately explained when the couple seeks the pastor's participation in their marriage.

Files

Keeping a separate file on each couple is imperative. This folder will serve as the repository for test results and other information, including completed homework assignments. The pastor's notes from each session should also be kept in this file. These are private and should be kept in a locked file cabinet.

Session notes

Session note-taking seems to be a great dilemma for some counselors. This is an entirely unnecessary struggle. Note-taking will enable the counselor to serve more effectively. This is sufficient reason for doing so. Counselees will seldom object. But if such an objection is raised, a simple explanation should be given. "I am taking notes to help me remember comments, facial expressions, problems mentioned, etc. This will help me to serve you better. You can be assured that these files are kept under lock and key." This explanation will usually calm their fears.

A format is suggested for this note-taking in Figure 1. Organized note-taking is helpful. This format is intended as an organizer. The use of both names can be especially useful if the couple or one of the individuals is not well known to the pastor-counselor. The date may provide a means for reconstruction of the order of events revealed in counseling. Let's say, for example, that Pastor George noted in the agenda column that Grace was very nervous during the third session. Thereafter, she exhibited an increase in nervous behavior whenever her mother was mentioned (also noted in agenda). During the sixth session Pastor George shared his observations with Grace and asked what had happened during the week of May 5 between her and her mother. She sat quietly and pondered an answer. Finally she said, "My mother accused me of immoral behavior with Jack!" This information enabled Pastor George to investigate the problem and teach Grace how to handle it properly.

The "Notes" portion of the sheet provides opportunity to record the general drift of the session. Some of these matters will be transferred to the agenda column as in the example above. The drift of a session includes such things as recounting

Figure 1
Premarital Counseling Session Record

Date _____

Name of man _____

Name of woman _____

Agenda

Notes

C/H	Homework Assign.
1.	
2.	
3.	
4.	
5.	

of a fight, events leading up to a certain climax, general information, particular events of past life, observations of the counselor, etc. Notes which will enable the counselor to reconstruct the session should be his objective.

The homework section is a record of assignments and an opportunity to check off successful completion (C/H = completed homework). This gives the counselor a reading of the couple's consistency at a glance.

Preparation for each session

Preparation for each session is advisable. A review of the last session and a transfer of agenda items to the note sheet of the day will keep the counselor current. He should be sure to have the homework sheets ready for distribution.

One further procedural factor should be mentioned. The couple should always be counseled together.[4] A good marriage requires the ability to communicate and the skill to discuss every conceivable legitimate subject must be cultivated. Premarital counseling is in reality part of the process of joining the man and the woman in holy matrimony. It takes two to join!

Charging a fee

Every pastor will have to determine for himself if he will charge a fee for this service. If a fee is to be charged, it should be cleared with the official board of the church.

A reasonable service charge may be made for the testing services. This can be distinguished from a counseling fee by designating the charge as a "testing fee" payable at the first session. This fee may include the cost of materials, the pastor's training, and the time involved.

I have found in some instances that charging a fee for counseling is an added incentive for the counselee to participate wholeheartedly in the sessions. The program suggested in this manual will demand from twelve to fifteen hours of a pastor's time. Computed at the minimum charge of $10 an hour plus testing fees, the pastor is offering $180 to $200 worth of counseling if he follows this manual. A $100 package fee for this program within the context of the pastoral ministry for nonmembers would be a reasonable figure. It could be suggested that this amount be given as a contribution to the church by nonmembers. I personally do not think that a pastor should charge fees to members. This counseling is primarily a ministry. It is for the investment of this time in ministry that the congregation is already paying him.

The Pastor-Counselor as "Knot-tier"

Nowhere does God command his shepherds to perform weddings. It is a good, acceptable, and, by implication, biblically warranted practice. But, it is not commanded. The pastor must evaluate the situation and determine guidelines for his practice. It seems to me that it is the pastor's prerogative to decide whom he will marry. It is a prerogative, however, not to be lightly exercised.

The first contingency which he should emphasize in a positive and gentle fashion is the mandatory completion of the premarital counseling program. When a couple approaches him to request his services, the pastor should assume that they are ready to at least appear for a private interview. When approached, he might simply produce his datebook and suggest a few alternate dates when they can come to his study to discuss the matter. At this meeting he can begin Session One of this program, which includes an explanation of this requirement.

During the course of the counseling the pastor may make the following recommendations:

1. He may suggest that the wedding be delayed (any number of reasons may come into play: parents' objections, immaturity of one or the other partner—spiritually and/or emotionally—etc.).
2. He may suggest termination of the relationship. For example, if attempts at evangelism fail, he must advise the believer to terminate the marriage plans.

In making either of these recommendations or in refusing to perform the ceremony, the pastor must exude a positive and gracious spirit. His reasoning must be carefully explained. His objective is to encourage the couple to consider his biblical concerns and restraint so that they will respond to them favorably.

When I counsel a young couple just graduating from Bible college or seminary who are planning to enter the ministry, I recommend that they postpone entering their field of service until September. Their ministry and their marriage will benefit from taking three months to focus on their relationship.

The Pastor-Counselor and Premarital Counseling for the Second Marriage

Assuming the couple is eligible for remarriage, there are three matters which demand particular attention. I estimate that almost half of my marital counseling experience has involved couples with at least one partner being remarried. Three items have been observed in many instances to be the focus of the marital discord. The order in which these are considered does not reflect their order of importance. This may vary from couple to couple.

Finances

The program will guide the pastor-counselor into the discussion of finances. However, it is geared toward the establishment of the first (hopefully the last) household. The special problem of the second marriage is the meshing of the independent financial status of each of the partners. Not infrequently, each will enter the marriage with a considerable bank account, land holdings, insurance, or an estate. In some cases a deceased husband will have left a trust fund which must remain in the woman's possession. These items should be thoroughly discussed by the couple and agreements for merging their means into common possession determined.[5] If merger is impossible because of legal complications, or must be stretched over several years for tax purposes, it would be well for the couple to write out their agreements. They should also be encouraged to have new wills drawn which carefully specify their wishes regarding financial matters. These should be drawn up in advance and become effective the day of the marriage. In regard to the details of these matters, the pastor should advise the couple to seek legal counsel.

One further matter should be discussed which falls into the category of financial concerns and may be emotionally charged. Should they live in the home of either party? The answer is not necessarily "no." But the wise pastor will explore this decision with them.

Many of these folks will be experienced at life. But there have been flaws somewhere in the cases of divorced people, or there would not have been a divorce. The pastor-counselor's interest is not so much in the details of the agreements worked out between the couple, but in their attitudes with respect to the establishment of oneness in this area.

Integration of families

Whether the couple is composed of a widow and widower or divorced people, family integration demands planning. Usually the couple will agree that the husband is the head of the home. He is ultimately responsible for biblical standards and discipline of children—even the woman's children from her previous marriage. It is this latter fact that requires special attention when standards and discipline are discussed. The pastor will need to adapt the program to meet this requirement. This is an excellent problem to approach by presenting an episode or two of role playing that is likely to elicit emotional responses which the couple will need to learn to handle in a spiritually mature manner.

The importance of cultivating a relationship with the other partner's children must be stressed. If children are involved, these people are marrying families, not just each other. It will take love, work, and time to facilitate a full family relationship. In cases involving children seven years of age and older (younger if the child has already had difficulty relating to the new mate), it is wise to have them attend at least one session. The counselor may probe anything he deems necessary, or he may simply observe the child's response to the parents during the session and determine further action in accordance with his observations.

While the status of legal adoption varies from state to state, it seems to me that legal adoption will have a favorable impact on family integration and should be encouraged in most instances.

There may be special problems (all boys on one side and all girls on the other) which will require creative approaches on the counselor's behalf. He and the parents will need to think together about the potential problems and work toward their prevention by planned integration.

Expectations

Each previously married individual brings with him or her expectations—usually more precisely defined expectations than those coming to marriage the first time—for the partner. This potential difficulty can be intensified for the widow or widower who has had a satisfying previous marriage. Instead of expecting the new mate to be like mother or dad, expectations will be for conformity to the previous mate.

Perhaps two suggestions can be shared with the couple after discussing this tendency:

1. Remember that your new mate is an individual. Allow him/her to be the person he/she is.
2. Agree to allow each other to freely express frustration when one of you feels pressed into a mold. The pressure will undoubtedly at times be unintentional; sometimes not. In either case, a previous commitment to discuss the issue will provide a framework for solving the problem.

The Pastor-Counselor and the Church

The pastor may effectively involve his congregation in this marital preparation. He may enlist couples, preferably those without children, whom he has counseled and who he is convinced have made a good marital adjustment, to be part of his team. When a couple comes for premarital counseling, they can be assigned to one of these couples. The team couple may have a weekly Bible study with them, develop a social relationship, and informally discuss any aspect of marriage adjustment which the counselee couple desires. This relationship can be continued for the first year of the marriage on a monthly basis. The pastor can adapt this idea and develop it to the extent that is practical in each situation.[6]

3

The Christian Concept
of an Equal Yoke

Out of my experience as a youth pastor, pastor, and counselor has grown a strong conviction that marrying another believer does not necessarily constitute being equally yoked. Just recently, for example, Mike came into my office to seek help for an ailing marriage. He and his wife, Nancy, were both believers. Mike wanted to become regularly involved in fellowship at a local assembly and reorder the family. Nancy, however, wished to continue a more worldly lifestyle. Mike was frustrated.

Recently, a seminary professor told me that some of the men in his seminary were there because their wives desired them to be. Others—like one case of my acquaintance, the husband moved from vocational Christian work to a secular vocation because of pressure from his wife—make crucial decisions changing the course of life on the basis of pressure from their mates.

Still others find their marriage to believers within a few years ending in divorce; or, if not divorce, great unhappiness when their mate's personality seems to change completely once they cross the threshold.

Something is drastically wrong. These folks have married on the basis that both professed to be Christians. Yet this "equal yoke" does not seem to yield a couple who are agreed and can walk together.

With these tragic facts in view, I should like to suggest that the pastor-counselor in his premarital counseling discern if there is truly an equal yoke. My concept of a truly equal yoke may be represented by four concentric circles (see figure 2). An equal yoke must begin with both parties professing faith in Christ. Their lifestyle should credit the profession. If the couple comes from different denominational or doctrinal backgrounds, it is wise to explore how they have dealt with these differences.

Figure 2
The Equal Yoke

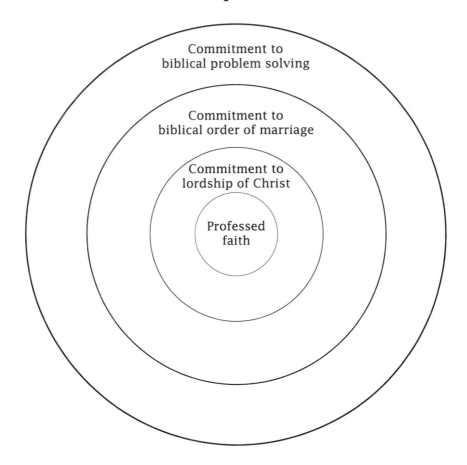

Commitment to
biblical problem solving

Commitment to
biblical order of marriage

Commitment to
lordship of Christ

Professed
faith

Secondly, the lordship of Christ must be a reality in their lives. If neither is committed to Christ's rule in their lives, there will be inevitable struggles. If one is and the other is not, this will yield conflict.

Thirdly, there should be a commitment to the biblical order of priorities in marriage. These are God, spouse, children, church, work, society. These should not be thought of as a strict order of descent. There are times within my ministry, for example, that I leave my family for extended periods of time. However, I plan for their management while away. I call and/or write regularly, and, when I return, I plan a special time with them to compensate for my absences.

Fourthly, there must be a commitment to work out problems biblically. This means a willing submission to the Word of God in every respect. It means I will talk with my spouse. I will share my feelings and struggles without using them to manipulate my mate. It means I will listen to (hear and consider) my mate. It means we will look together for biblical principles regarding our problems and will subject ourselves to them.

The premarital counselor will do well to keep this diagram in mind and ask himself, "Is this couple truly equally yoked?" Remember, Amos asks, "Can two walk together, except they be agreed?" (Amos 3:3).

4

Exposition of the Marriage Ceremony: Dearly Befuddled

W. Wilson Benton

I am delighted that my good friend and colleague, Dr. Benton, has agreed to allow me to include the following chapter. While I served on his staff at Kirk of the Hills Presbyterian Church in St. Louis, he was a regular feature in our Premarital Preparation Program. His presentation of this material was entertaining and instructive. I believe it will enhance this book and your understanding of the marriage ceremony.

The statements that begin the marriage ceremony remind us of the theology of marriage.[1] *Instituted by God, regulated by his commandments, blessed by our Lord Jesus Christ, to be held in honor among all men.* As we think about those phrases, we are reminded of the nature and character of marriage as God has established it. He is the one who invented it. It was his idea, not ours. We might like to claim that love leading to marriage is of human origin, but actually it is of divine origin. God is the one who said, "It is not good that man should be alone; I will make him a help meet for him." He is the God of sexuality. The charge leveled by unbelievers against believers is that the latter's view of sex and sexuality is

47

Victorian and puritanical when in fact nothing could be further from the truth. The God of the Christian is the God who created us male and female, making sexuality possible and making marriage possible. He is to be honored and praised for this gift of his love to the human race.

Marriage is to be "regulated by his commandments." Since, therefore, God is the author of marriage, the inventor of marriage, and the instituter of marriage, he is the one who knows how marriage should function.

We see people taking the great gift of sexuality and using it according to their own desires and lust rather than receiving the gift from the giver and using it according to his instruction. The Bible, in a sense, is the owner's manual. It is the manufacturer's book of instructions and with the gift God has given us instructions as to how we are to use the gift. It is important that we study not human psychology first, nor human desires first, nor biological drives first, but that we study God's Word first to understand how we are to conduct ourselves in the glorious relationship of marriage instituted by God and regulated by his commandments. It is an expression of our love to keep his commandments. Or to put it another way, keeping God's commandments is the best way of showing love. For instance, when the Bible says to Christians in general, "speak the truth to one another," that surely applies to the Christian husband and Christian wife. Or when the Bible says to Christians in general, "Be tender-hearted, forgiving one another," that certainly applies to the Christian husband and Christian wife. All of the relational instructions (commandments) of Scripture have specific application in marriage as two people work to express their love for each other.

Marriage is a social institution. It is an expression of God's common grace to the human race. As a minister I am free to marry non-Christians as well as Christians. The Bible prevents me from marrying a Christian and a non-Christian, but I can marry two non-Christians because this expression of God's grace is not limited to his people. It is given to the human race at large—"to be held in honor among all men." We, in our living, in our relationships, in our businesses, should never do anything that would harm the marriage relationship of any people . . . not just ourselves but any couples anywhere.

Marriage has been "blessed by our Lord Jesus Christ." We remember his first miracle performed at a wedding ceremony. He was there to place his blessings on the marriage of two people.

The Lord, from Genesis right through Revelation, indicates his blessing on marriage. In Genesis we are told that man should not live alone: "It is not good that man should be alone; I will make him an help meet for him." In the Book of Revelation, the relationship still stands. We have the marriage feast of the Lamb described for us. Jesus is pictured as the bridegroom and the church is pictured as his bride. The relationship which God himself chose to illustrate the relationship of Christ to the church is the marriage relationship. Of all the thousands of relationships he might have chosen, the one he selected was the relationship of husband and wife. "Husbands, love your wives as Christ loved the church." "Wives, submit yourselves to your husbands as the church is submissive to Christ." Not only has he blessed this relationship in terms of things physical but also in terms of things spiritual. In fact, we are told in the ceremony that marriage is for the welfare and happiness of mankind. Here is the greatest foretaste of heaven we have on earth and every relationship of marriage should be for the benefit, the blessing, the well-being, the growth, the development, the progress of the two people being married.

I always ask the couple before me, "Will she be a better person because you are marrying her?" "Will he be a better person because you are marrying him?" And I can always predict the answer. If I ask him, "Will she be better because you are marrying her?" he will always say, "Well, *I* certainly will be." That's the standard answer, but that is not the answer to my question. My question is this: "Will *she* be better because you are marrying her?" We must put aside our false humility and in all honesty say before God, "I believe she will be better because I am marrying her." If you do not believe that, then please, for God's sake, don't marry her! It must be for her well-being, it must be for her benefit, it must be for her spiritual growth and development that you marry her. The same is true for the wife. She must be able to say in all honesty but with all humility before God, "He will be better because I am marrying him." In other words, we are to bring out the best in each other. We are to compensate for the weaknesses. Love covers a multitude of sins. We are to cover up the blemishes, the shortcomings, the deficiencies in one another and highlight the strengths and help develop the gifts in our spouses. If we are not doing this then we are not fulfilling the purpose of marriage in our relationship. God designs that it be for the welfare and the happiness of mankind. So from time to time we need to ask ourselves some pointed, personal, and searching questions. Is my spouse better because he or she is married to me? Am I doing all within my power to promote the welfare of that person? Again the passages of Scripture that call for this among

Christians certainly are applicable to the marriage relationship. When Paul says, "Look not every man after his own interest but also to the interest of others," surely that applies to the husband as he looks after the interest of the wife. Surely that applies to the wife as she looks after the interest of her husband.

In this regard it is also helpful to remember that God has selected your mate and done so specifically with your own personality in mind, with your own gifts in mind but at the same time with your own deficiencies in mind. He knows that one who will best compensate, who will best serve your well-being; therefore it is only wise that we seek his will in this regard. Again the passages of Scripture that speak generally of searching for God's will and seeking his direction apply specifically to the choice of a life mate.

Instituted by God, regulated by his commandments, blessed by our Lord Jesus Christ, held in honor among all men, established for the welfare and happiness of mankind. Our Savior has declared that a man should leave his father and mother and cleave unto his wife. Here is the word of instruction that comes from the Book of Genesis and is reiterated by Christ in his earthly ministry. It is interesting that he does not say that the wife is to leave her father and mother and cleave unto her husband, but rather instructs the husband to leave his father and mother and cleave unto his wife. There is a good reason for this: the husband needs to establish a degree of independence. He needs to be able to care for his wife, to make provisions for her needs and so become the head of the family. If he is not able to leave his father and mother in this sense, he is not prepared financially, emotionally, psychologically, or vocationally to cleave unto his wife. Questions need to be asked about the financial stability of the couple as they seek your counsel in marriage. Will they be able to maintain their home independently of the support of the parental groups, either the bride's or the groom's parents?

The instructions continue with these phrases: *By his apostles he has instructed those who enter into this relationship to cherish a mutual esteem in love, to bear each other's infirmities and weaknesses, to comfort each other in sorrow, in sickness, and in trouble.* Such contingencies are a part of life. We must expect them. It would be foolish to suppose that love will be expressed without these pressures. The question is, "Are we prepared to love each other through such circumstances? Are we honestly ready to provide for each other and our households, to pray for and encourage each other in the things which pertain to God; to live together as heirs of grace?"

While it is true that marriage is a social institution and an expression of God's common grace and that two unbelievers may be married, it is also true that only those who are Christians will know the fulness of joy which this relationship is designed to bring. Only as couples learn to pray for each other and encourage each other in the things which pertain to God, only as they live together in spiritual harmony can they establish the kind of marriage relationship that will produce divinely intended joy.

This is the first paragraph in the introductory statement on the doctrine of marriage and basically what it says is this: God approves of marriage. God is the author of marriage, the institutor of marriage, the regulator of marriage, the one who blesses marriage. He is the one who gives us the grace necessary to fulfill our vows. He is the one who enables us to overlook faults and to grant forgiveness. Without God marriage is possible, but without God marriage is not profitable or pleasant as he intends it to be.

Now the second paragraph in the opening statement of the doctrine of marriage addresses the congregation. The old form of the question was this: *Is there any person present who knows any just cause why these two may not be lawfully joined together in marriage; if so, I require him to make it known or ever after hold his peace.* Of course, that statement has been the object of many a joke. What will the preacher do if someone jumps up and says, "Yoo hoo, I do." Or what will the bride do when some guy jumps up and says, "Yes, may I have a word?" Or what will the groom do if some cute thing third row back waves her handkerchief and says, "May I speak to the congregation?" That is the reason that many choose to leave this statement out of the ceremony, but actually it is included for a good purpose. In the first place, it acknowledges the presence of the congregation. You have invited friends and relatives to come and you want them to participate in the ceremony. Here is a way of your acknowledging their presence. They are addressed with this question.

But beyond that, the second thing this question does is pledge them to your support. True, the pledge comes in a negative form and the question is answered by silence, but it is nonetheless an expression of the congregation's support of and encouragement to the couple. *Does any person know why they may not lawfully join in marriage? If not, ever after hold your peace.* This is a way of saying, "Don't undermine them, don't talk about them, don't put stumbling blocks in their way; do everything you can to help them, support them, and encourage this couple in their relationship."

Third, it is a way of saying to the congregation, "We want your help and we need it. We are very much in love. We believe we are going to have the best marriage that has ever been. At the same time we know it is a working relationship and we need you; we need your prayers, we need your support, we need your counsel and advice and while we must establish our own home, we know we cannot do it without the loving encouragement and support from our friends and our neighbors. That's why you are here." So for these reasons the question is good.

At the same time I believe there may be a better way of accomplishing the same end, and that is with the use of a responsive reading at this point in the ceremony.[2] Of course, a bulletin is required if this is done because the reading needs to be printed. The minister can read a statement and the congregation can respond. It makes the pledge of support more positive because it is clearly stated rather than indicated by silence. I think this is a better way, but if the couple chooses not to use a bulletin and you don't have the privilege of printing the responsive reading, I still feel very strongly that the question to the congregation needs to be addressed; (1) to acknowledge them; (2) to pledge their support, and (3) to have the couple confess even by having this item in their marriage ceremony that they need the support of these people.

God approves of marriage and we believe God approves of this specific marriage. That is the first paragraph of the ceremony. The second paragraph says that all of these friends and relatives approve of the marriage. The third paragraph in the opening statement about the doctrine of marriage addresses the couple. *I charge both of you before the great God and searcher of all hearts that if either of you knows any reason you may not lawfully be joined together in marriage you do now confess it; for be well assured that if persons are joined otherwise than God's Word allows, this union is not blessed by him.* This question may seem a bit perfunctory and a bit pointless because they are standing before the minister and he is asking if they want to be married. Well, obviously they would not be standing there if they did not want to be married, but again, there are purposes behind the question. It impresses on the congregation the solemnity with which they are entering this relationship. It reminds them that this is not a decision lightly made on their part; that they have in fact searched the Word of God; that they have discerned the will of God as clearly as they can and they believe he would have them to be married. In fact, that is the positive statement here and, again, it is expressed in a negative way and answered in silence but it is a way of saying we believe it is God's will for them to be married.

There is a sense in which every couple should be able to say, "We had to get married." Understandably in our culture that implies immorality; that implies sex before marriage which has resulted in pregnancy; therefore, we had to get married. But in a higher and holier sense every couple should say, "We had to get married. We believe it is God's will for us to be married. In fact, we believe that we would be sinning against God if we did not get married. It is not a matter of choice for us, it is a matter of obedience. God has called us to this relationship with each other and we would be going contrary to his will if we do not unite in marriage. We had to get married." In a sense that is the meaning of this implied question. *I charge you to search your hearts to see if there is any reason you may not lawfully be joined together in marriage.* The positive side is, "Yes, we should be, we must be, we have to be married." So the third paragraph says the couple is in favor of marriage and this particular marriage.

Now the stage has been set with these three words of introduction: (1) God established it, he's in favor of marriage and he's in favor of this marriage. God is prepared to put his blessing on this relationship. (2) All the friends and neighbors and relatives present approve of the marriage, and (3) The couple is standing before the minister to say that they believe this is God's will; they want to get married. So there comes now a prayer, the prayer of invocation invoking the blessing of God upon the ceremony. The minister performs the ceremony. He does not perform the marriage. Only God performs the marriage. He is the only one who can take two people and of them make one new person. The minister is the representative of God on that occasion and it is a great privilege for him to perform the ceremony; but he, of all people, recognizes that he cannot perform the marriage. It is a mystery when God takes two people and makes of them one new person. The prayer of invocation is a prayer to God that he will come and do just that. It is an expression of God's providence in the lives of the couple, preparing them throughout all of their lives to this point. Everything that has happened to them has prepared them to be the spouse of the other. Everything that has happened in terms of family background and training and upbringing, and schooling, and education, and dating relationships, all of those things in the providence of God had been used to prepare the spouse for the other.

There is a sense of awe which should accompany the couple as they present themselves to God saying, "We stand before you as miracle material asking you to take us now and to bind us together." The prayer indicates that God will take the two and make one and I would encourage the couple to prepare for that kind of glorious and mysterious event which somehow transpires in the wedding ceremony.

There is something missing by God's design when couples simply live together and do not present themselves before God for the service of marriage. Something actually takes place in that ceremony itself which does not take place apart from the ceremony. I am not sure that I understand all that is involved at this point, but I believe that God is present in a very special way to take the lives of two people and blend them together in a way he will not do when people outside of marriage simply take up the business of "living together," as we say in our culture.

Now if it is true that this takes place in the marriage ceremony, I would encourage the couple to anticipate the ceremony itself. So often we see that as a necessary evil through which we must pass to get on with the business of living together. Such is not the case. It ought to be anticipated as a great blessing in and of itself. Preparations should be made in every possible way for the ceremony. Though it is brief, the consequences last for the rest of our lives here on this earth! Surely, then, we should prepare for that ceremony. Now if God takes two and blends them together, then I encourage the couple to name the relationship. I encourage them to think about the relationship being born that day as a tiny baby—a baby relationship; and it will help them to personify that relationship if they name it. The first few days and weeks and months of a baby's life are the most crucial. The baby needs more attention then than at any other time in his life, and so with a baby relationship. That baby relationship will grow and develop. It will not be treated at age ten as it is treated at ten days of age, and so with a baby. I ask them to draw parallels in their mind between the raising of a baby and the raising of a relationship. To help them to do that I encourage them to name the relationship and we begin to talk about the relationship.

It is obvious you do not live for yourself in marriage. It is true you do not live for the other in marriage. Basically, the two live for the new one person being created by the marriage. You live for your corporate personality, your corporate relationship, not really for each other. That relationship is to become supreme in the spending of time and effort and energy in the relationship of marriage. What an exciting thing to realize that God has brought the two of you together in the miracle of marriage, taking two lives and blending them together to form one new life.

After the prayer come the questions of intent. That is precisely what they indicate: their intentions. You say you love each other. How do you love each other? What is the manner in which you pledge yourselves to love each other? That is really the force of these questions. The question is this: _____, *will you take _____ to be your wife, and will you pledge yourself to her in all love and honor, in all duty and service, in all faith and tenderness, to live with her and cherish her according to the ordinance of God in the holy bond of marriage?* Allow me to make several observations about the question. It says you are giving yourself away. Will you take so and so to be your wife and will you pledge yourself to her? Actually, all you have is yourself; you cannot offer her your wealth; that may be gone tomorrow. You cannot offer her dreams and hopes and ambitions and expectations; there is no substance to that; so basically, all you can offer her is who you are; and you are saying, "I am ready to give myself away 100 percent. No strings attached, without reservations, all that I am, all that I have, all that I hope to be, I'm willing to give to you." The question is reciprocal for the bride about the groom. She is saying the same thing, "I can only give you myself, but I give you the entirety, the totality of my being." That is a scary thought. If you are not ready to give yourself away totally and completely to another person you are not ready for marriage.

Marriage is not fifty/fifty. Marriage is one hundred/one hundred. Each person giving himself 100 percent to the other person and that is in essence the thrust of this question. Will you pledge yourself to the other? If you are not tired of being the person you are then you are not ready to get married. You cannot remain as you are and be married. You are giving yourself away. The other person has control over you, can make demands on you, has the right to expect things from you and if you are not ready to enter into that kind of self-denying relationship then you are not ready to be married. So we ask: "Is this your intention? Is this the way you plan to love each other? Will you pledge yourself to him or her?"

Then follows a series of three couplets, all of which are important and significant. "Will you pledge yourself to him/her in love and honor?" Those words are not redundant. It is one thing to love a person; it's another thing to honor a person. I have some high school friends whom I love, but I do not honor them. I love them because of past associations and friendships but I do not really respect them because they have not done much with their lives and they have wasted talents and gifts and abilities. They have not been productive human beings, but I still love them. On the other hand, I honor the mayor of St. Louis, but I do not love him. I respect him and his position, but I would hardly say that I have deep affection for him. Now the point of the question is this: will you blend these two things together in your marriage? There are marriages where people can love each other but do not really respect each other, do not honor each other, do not hold each other in regard, do not have high esteem for one another. There is some kind of self-oriented love, but there is no honor. On the other hand there are relationships where people honor one another but they do not really love each other. They respect each other, they give due regard to one another, but the warmth and glow of affection is missing. It is not either love or honor, honor or love—it is love and honor. Affection and respect are to be blended together in the proper marriage relationship. Is it your intention to love each other in this way?

Then the second couplet: love and honor, duty and service. It is one thing to perform our services as husbands and wives. We have duties and obligations and we must perform those. They are not pleasant. It is not fun to take out the garbage; it is not fun to wash the dishes; it is not fun to mow the grass; it is not fun to wash the clothes. Each spouse has a list of services that must be performed so that the marriage relationship will function and life will be productive. But beyond this service which is inherent in the relationship, there are duties that, as we say, are beyond the call—service beyond the call of duty and we need to be sure we are doing the *extra* things as well as the *expected* things. Again it is not either this or that, it is both. I do those things that are expected, those things that are inherent in my job description. Those things that are inherent in my job description as a wife or husband, but above and beyond that I render service to the spouse in those extra special things, things that are not required, things that are not inherent, perhaps even things that are not expected. I find delight in doing that. And so the question, "What is your intention?" How do you intend to love each other? In duty and service?

And then the third couplet: in faith and tenderness. We are told today that you can be very, very tender but not very faithful. You can be tender here and tender there and tender elsewhere but not faithful; on the other hand you can be faithful but not be very tender. Live under one roof, share the same bed, never violate the sanctity of the marriage relationship in any sexual immorality and yet not very tender. Again it is not either/

or—either faithfulness or tenderness, but faithfulness and tenderness, tenderness and faithfulness. Hence the question of intent: Is this how you intend to love each other? In love and honor, in duty and service, in faith and tenderness?

Now, when these questions have been answered in the affirmative, perhaps the last person in all the world to be convinced that this marriage is proper is now convinced. That is the father of the bride. Up until this point he has been standing between the bride and the groom. He has heard the Scripture to support the belief that God is in favor of marriage; he has heard the people say they are in favor of this marriage; the couple is standing before him ready to be married; he has heard them express their intentions of exactly how they are going to love each other; and so now a question is addressed to him—"Who gives the bride to be married to the groom?" He says whatever the bride tells him to say. Basically two responses are most common: (1) "I do," or (2) "Her mother and I."

There is something that perhaps you would want to institute in the marriage ceremony at this point and that is a question to the parents after the questions of intent but before the giving of the bride. You might want to consider having both sets of parents stand and address first the parents of the groom with a question like this, "Your son to whom you gave birth and whom you nourished and supported and brought to the fullness of manhood stands before you today expressing his desire to have _____ as his wife. Will you place your blessings on their marriage and will you receive _____ into your own home and family and treat her as your very own daughter?" And then you address the parents of the bride with basically the same question. "Your daughter whom God has created through your love for each other stands before you in the beauty of womanhood expressing her desire to have _____ as her husband. Will you place your blessing on their marriage and will you receive him into your home and family and treat him as your very own son?"

Then would follow the question of the giving of the bride. At this point there is a major break in the ceremony and you usually move from one level to a higher level, if there are steps involved. The wedding party follows the minister as he moves behind the kneeling bench and you move to the heart and core of the marriage ceremony. Actually a marriage ceremony does not climax at the end; the climax comes in the middle. It builds up to a pinnacle and then from that pinnacle it moves down to the conclusion. Of course the pinnacle is the exchanging of vows between the bride and the groom.

Just a couple of words about the vows. I encourage couples to write their vows using the traditional vows as a basis, but with the counsel and advice of the minister, who maintains veto power. There are certain elements which need to be involved in any vow: (1) the element of commitment—total, complete, unreserved commitment; (2) the element of continuation . . . there is no time limit set on the vow apart from death itself; (3) the element of circumstances and you want to say whatever the circumstances, love will be maintained; (4) the fourth element has to do with the covenant concept. A vow is a covenant made primarily with God first, addressed to God and through God to the spouse.

If these four elements are maintained, the vow can be expressed in a number of different ways. The traditional vow says, *"I _____ take you _____ to be my wedded wife."* This vow is a reference to the covenantal relationship into which each is now entering. Here we are picking up the language out of the questions of intent—love and honor, duty and service, faith and tenderness—before God.

I do promise and covenant before God and these witnesses to be your loving and faithful husband. Reference is made back to the concept of marriage being instituted by God, that marriage is the expression of a covenantal relationship ("I . . . covenant"), that the marriage vow is first made to God and only in a secondary sense to the spouse. The language reflects the question of intent. Not all the phrases are repeated, but the first and last couplets are echoed—"loving and faithful" husband.

Then follow a series of couplets describing in a general sense the circumstances of life in which the love relationship of marriage will be nurtured *in plenty and in want, in joy and in sorrow, in sickness and in health.*

Basically the vow says that whatever the circumstances, we will love one another. Our love will not follow the roller coaster pattern of circumstances. Our love was not born of circumstances and our love will not be controlled by circumstances. Actually our love came from above and so is maintained on a level above the circumstances. Couples should never say in response, when asked how they are doing, "Very well under the circumstances." They are not to be living under the circumstances but above the circumstances. If you can think of an illustration, the line of love is above the up and down line charting the circumstances in which we live. While we may want only a bed of roses, life does not promise that. There will be plenty and there will be want, there will be joy and there will be sorrow, there will be sickness as well as health; but this is not to impact our love.

The vow is also stating that God's love is the only love that is strong enough to maintain our marriage relationship. My love for my spouse is not my love for my spouse, but basically is God's love for my spouse channelled through me. I am privileged to serve as a channel through which God expresses his love to this person who happens to be my spouse and all of this is implied in the vow. I think there is one other thing that is implied here, and perhaps even can be stated if the vow is rewritten, and that is the dependence on God we must acknowledge for the strength necessary to fulfill the vow we say we covenant before God. I think the implication is that as we make the covenant to him so we receive the promise from him, the grace that is necessary to perform the vows.

There are other things that can be added, other expressions that may be used to communicate these concepts, but no one of these concepts may be omitted. All four of them are absolutely essential if in fact the vow constitutes a vow.

After the vow comes the reading of Scripture. Usually a portion of 1 Corinthians 13 is read with an introductory statement indicating that this is the biblical description of the love that the two have just expressed. Again a reminder that God's power is the only power that can enable us to fulfill the vow and maintain the marriage relationship.

After the reading of the Scripture there may be the exchange of rings . . . the symbolism is usually obvious though at times it may be stated.

After the rings perhaps the lighting of the unity candle and/or the celebration of the Lord's Supper if there is a desire to do so. Only one or the other of these, not both, is used and neither is essential to the essence of the marriage ceremony; but the couples may choose to include these elements in the ceremony.

The pastoral prayer should be just that—a pastoral prayer for the couple. The prayer is followed by the pronouncement of marriage. This may be followed by a charge based on Ephesians 5 addressed to the husband and wife. And, here, while this is not expressed in the ceremony, I think it is good to share with the couple the idea that their relationship is to be evangelistic in nature. If someone were to say, "Exactly how does Christ love me," I should be able to say, "Look at (Jack) and (Mary) who just got married. See how he loves her; that is how Jesus loves the church." This is the great illustration that God himself has chosen. We should be communicating to the world in flesh and blood the invisible ways Christ loves the church. Of course, it is an argument from the lesser to the greater and ours is an imperfect love and his is a perfect love but nonetheless the pattern stands. We should be loving our wives as Christ loved the church and gave himself for it and Christian marriages should be that ever present illustration to which people can point and say, "This is the way that Jesus loves his bride the church." On the other hand if someone says, "How am I to live as a Christian? How am I to acknowledge the Lordship of Christ? How am I to submit?" one should point to the marriage relationship. "Do you know (Jack) and (Mary) who just got married? If so, see how she supports her husband? See how she submits to her husband?" Here is the way in which the church is to submit to Jesus the bridegroom.

The ceremony closes with the benediction and the presentation of the couple as husband and wife to the congregation. A great time of rejoicing! And a great time it should be!

Illustration 1

Minister: We have assembled in this service of worship with Robert and Tamela to affirm our love for them by sharing in the celebration of their marriage; and to witness the taking of their vows before God.

Congregation: As friends and loved ones, we gather with them in this time of celebration which is both joyous and solemn. We rejoice that our heavenly father has brought them together. We rejoice in their experience of love. We affirm their desire and God-given right to be joined together in marriage.

Minister: Robert and Tamela have invited us to witness their joining in covenant relationship.

Congregation: As both friends and witnesses, we pledge our support in their leaving their families and in their establishing a new and independent family unit.

Minister: We pledge both corporately and individually to pay Robert and Tamela the debt of love.

Congregation: As those who share the common weakness of mankind, we affirm our commitment to love them and to reserve judgment. We pledge our intent to respect the integrity of their individual relationship while at the same time we affirm our commitment to come to their rescue if we "see them overtaken in a fault."[3]

PART
TWO

Program for
Premarital Counseling

5

Session One

A couple may be introduced to this program by a summary of the biblical basis for premarital counseling, emphasizing that the counseling will center on the Lord Jesus Christ and the Word of God. This can accomplish four things:

1. It will establish the God-derived authority for the process.
2. It will communicate an attitude of hope that this experience will indeed be of value.
3. It will build involvement by communicating a genuine concern for the couple and a sense of responsibility on the pastor's part for their marital well-being.
4. If the couple is unfamiliar with the pastor, this will clearly identify his perspective to them.

The program should then be gone over in synoptic form. Highlighting some aspects of the program and illustrating a few of those with which the counselor notes one or the other of the candidates identifying can build interest and excitement. The time commitment to seven sessions of ninety minutes in length should be explained. Also, since this program depends on the couple's involvement in the process through homework assignments, the pastor should gain a definite commitment from the prospective counselees to complete each unit of work before returning to the next session.

The pastor-counselor should set forth his goals for the premarital counseling. He may want to use such a broad statement as, "I'm not in the business of performing weddings; I'm in the business of establishing Christian homes."[1] Perhaps the articulation of a number of specific goals corresponding to the vital areas of life which are going to be discussed in the course of the program would be profitable. The manner of handling this matter is not as important as the fact. When the reader has completed this section, a good exercise would consist of writing out the goals for each session as he sees them.

If the couple gives any hint of having experienced difficulties in their relationship, the pastor should establish hope and work to elicit a commitment to solving these problems during the counseling. One or the other may have come for this initial session under duress. They need hope! They need assurance that the counselor will take the problems seriously. They need confidence that the problems can be solved and their marriage need not begin on a negative note. Many times such situations can be handled parallel to the regular program with little additional time invested.

Another first session attitude, which underscores the necessity of a careful delineation of the program, is illustrated by the comment of one of the young men who participated in my premarital counseling project. He said, "I was very reluctant to become involved in premarital counseling. My fiancée and I had had some rough times, and I was afraid that the counseling might further damage our relationship. You convinced me in the first session to continue, and the counseling has helped us work out many of these problems." Some couples will come to that first session because they are convinced that premarital counseling is the right thing to do, or because they have a glimmer of hope that the pastor can do something to help them improve their relationship. If in that first session the counselor clearly gives such individuals hope, they will become enthusiastically involved in the process as did the young man referred to above.

When writing about the first session of a series of counseling sessions, Adams cogently remarks, "The first session is particularly important. Basic trends are set; initial attitudes and decisions, as well as relationships, are formed by both the counselor and the counselees."[2] What Adams has written about the first session especially applies to what I have termed "Introductory Remarks."

Determine the Eligibility of the Couple

It is important to determine the eligibility of the couple for marriage. Though God has ordained marriage for all mankind, he nowhere has commanded pastors to perform marriage ceremonies. However, by implication it is incumbent on a pastor not to join together a couple in God's name who, on the basis of God's Word, is ineligible for such a Christian blessing.[3]

There are four questions which a pastor should ask. The proper answers to these questions will qualify the couple to continue the premarital program.

1. Have both of you been born again?

No doubt there are a few conservative pastors who would not ask this question. They clearly recognize that to marry outside the Lord is to violate God's commandment.[4] Having gained a simple answer of "yes" to this question does not, however, automatically obligate the pastor to marry the couple. He should inform them that if at any time during the counseling he discovers good cause to recommend that they do not marry, he will exercise his prerogative not to perform the ceremony.[5]

The counselor might discover during the counseling attitudes toward God or others which will make it impossible for one or the other of the couple to make a well-adjusted marriage partner so long as he or she refuses to be submissive toward God and correct this problem. As the counseling progresses, the pastor may uncover other reasons for which he cannot perform the wedding "of faith" (Rom. 14:23). These, of course, should be very serious in nature and explicitly explained to the couple. In the final analysis, he is responsible to God for agreeing or refusing to perform the marriage.

Though it was implied above, let it be stated with clarity that no pastor may qualify a believer and an unbeliever for marriage. To do so is to aid and abet a most severe act of disobedience on the part of the believer.[6]

There appears to be as much disunity among evangelicals regarding the question of marrying two unbelievers as there is unity concerning the joining of two believers. Some have argued that since the pastor acts as an agent of the state as well as of the church in performing a wedding, he can officiate at the unbelievers' wedding in this capacity. Others, correctly recognizing that marriage is ordained of God for all humans, find no difficulty in accommodating two unbelievers. Some pastors will perform a private ceremony based on this same logic, but refuse

to provide a church wedding. A careful survey would undoubtedly disclose other variations of affirmative argumentation. This
was confirmed by a survey conducted by one of my students in
a pastoral counseling seminar. He discovered that nine out of
ten evangelical pastors questioned did marry unbelievers.

The pastor must give careful consideration to the nature of
his participation in a wedding and the nature of a Christian wedding. When a pastor consents to perform a wedding for two
unbelievers, whether in private or public, he is giving credence
to whatever incorrect motives and concepts about Christianity
that brought these individuals to him as a representative of God.

A Christian wedding is at least two things. It is the entering
into a covenant relationship whose framework pertains especially to believers—the pronouncing of the man and the woman
as husband and wife in the name of the triune God. The marriage ceremony is also worship, both on the part of the participants and the observers. Every pastor will have to take cog-
nizance of these facts before God when he considers marrying
two unbelievers.

2. Has either of you any secrets that should be shared?

Marriage is the most intimate of all human relationships. It
must be built on honesty. If there are past actions or activities
which may surface at a later date and cause disruption of the
relationship, they should be disclosed frankly at this time. The
counselor may sense reluctance on the part of one or the other
of the partners when this subject is broached. If so, he should
carefully explain that, though suppressed at the present time,
guilt over remaining silent may force the person to confess this
at a later date, creating an unnecessary difficulty. Such an explanation may encourage the sharing of the discomforting secret.
Even if a sense of guilt does not force a confession, there is
always the possibility that someone may intentionally or unin-
tentionally raise the issue or that some future legal formality
may bring the unwanted revelation. The pastor will do well to
emphasize the responsibility of Christian love to speak the
truth.[7]

Some issues which fall into this category are as follows: (a) a
police record or jail sentence and the reason for either, (b)
responsibility for an illegitimate child, (c) previous sexual experiences, (d) homosexual practice, (e) victim of rape, (f) an abortion, (g) sterility, (h) incest, (i) medical difficulty, etc.

Frequently, one of the couple will be grateful for the opportunity to reveal such a situation in the presence of the counselor.

This context assures the person the best possible atmosphere to exercise, in many cases, an already existent desire to share such a matter with a prospective mate. No pastor-counselor can afford to miss this propitious occasion.

3. Has either of you been divorced?

In the same survey cited above, the student found that nine out of ten evangelical pastors indicated divorce as their main condition for not marrying two believers. Certainly the pastor must ascertain if either of the couple has been divorced, so that he can properly proceed. But he cannot, as has been the practice of evangelical Protestantism on the whole, simply refuse them God's blessing on that bare fact of divorce. The situation can never determine theology. Therefore, it may be imperative that the pastor who would honor God rethink his position on this issue. The growing divorce rate in general and among believers in particular demands that every pastor know his position. But the situation does not determine his position, theology does. What he must do is ask himself if his theology and policy are biblically derived or culturally conditioned by the tradition of his fathers.

No one has written more persuasively or perspicaciously with regard to this issue than Jay Adams. Therefore, I have taken the liberty to quote him at length. Adams writes:

> More and more today the pastor will encounter divorced persons seeking remarriage. Many, if not most of these divorces, he will discover, were not obtained on biblical grounds (adultery, desertion of a believer by an unbeliever). Even when grounds may have been biblical, the manner in which the issues were handled (exercise of church discipline, attitudes, attempts at reconciliation, etc.), may not have been proper. *Before proceeding to perform any second marriage . . . be sure that all matters in the past have been settled biblically.* In most cases, the pastor will find that there are still loose ends that must be tied up biblically. He must not move ahead until these have been settled. He must warn, urge and encourage. 1 Corinthians 7:27–28 clearly speaks of remarriage. Paul here writes of a man properly "loosed from a wife" . . . remarrying without sin. . . . It is wrong therefore, for a pastor to counsel that there is no case in which remarriage is possible. To hold to such a position is to try to be more pious than Paul. Indeed, in 1 Corinthians 6:9–11 he assures us that one can be washed and entirely cleansed, *even of adultery.* When this has happened, what God has cleansed, no man has the right to call unclean.

On the one hand, therefore, it is essential not to qualify those whom God disqualifies because of previous marital obligations. Fundamentally they are those who have not done all that the Scriptures require in order to put the past entirely into the past by reconciliation, church discipline, or whatever obligations yet remain. But when, according to God's Word there is an official statement on the minute book of the board of a disciplining Bible believing congregation to the effect that the party (or parties) concerned has done all required to satisfy God and man and that the matter is closed, qualifying him (or her) for remarriage, no evangelical pastor should refuse to remarry the person. On the other hand, no minister *on his own* should undertake to determine the matter; it must be resolved by the church, acting officially in Christ's name.[8]

Having determined that his stance is biblical, the pastor will have to deal with each situation on its own merits and counsel the couple accordingly.[9]

4. Are there any parental objections to this marriage?

This question may not always be applicable. If not, the couple's answer will make this obvious. In most cases a Christian couple will answer in the negative. But there are times when an affirmative answer will be forthcoming. This question is important for three reasons: (a) Children are commanded (Eph. 6) to honor their parents. (b) Every couple is to a degree marrying a mate's family. He will have to learn to relate to them and they to him or her. If that family is opposed to the marriage and the couple proceeds, they will be constructing a wall between family members. (c) An unnecessary strain will be placed on the marriage. There will be an inevitable determination to prove the objecting family to have been wrong.

The pastor must explore with the couple the objections of the family. He may consider asking the family, even in some cases both families, to come to the counseling session to discuss the issues involved. If the objections of the family are legitimate, the pastor may have to recommend to the couple that they postpone the wedding until the objections can be resolved. All the possible ramifications of such a situation cannot be discussed here, but the necessity to pursue this question and the issues that may arise is clear.

In the majority of cases, the pastor will be able to qualify the couple within a relatively short time with little or no problem. He should be prepared, in the cases that warrant it, to refuse to continue the program of counseling until the couple has grappled with the issues at hand. He should offer assistance through counseling to bring a resolution to the problem.

Administer the Taylor-Johnson Temperament Analysis Test

The use of the T-JTA test does require certain credentials. These may be obtained by most seminary graduates or duly ordained and qualified ministers who secure ten hours of training through the distributor. Interested men usually will be able to find someone in their area qualified to provide the training.[10]

This test does not purpose to be Christian. But it is not generally offensive to biblical presuppositions. Some may desire that certain questions be worded differently; however, overall the average pastor will find this test a helpful tool for surfacing potential problem areas between prospective mates.[11]

The T-JTA is designed to serve as a quick and efficient method of measuring certain personality traits which influence personal, social, marital, and family adjustment. It is a paper and pencil test that may be administered to an individual, to couples, or to groups.[12] According to the manual, the test is designed to provide an evaluation in visual form showing a person's concept of himself.[13]

The T-JTA serves not only as a diagnostic instrument, but the Shaded Profile frequently is used as a tool in the actual counseling process. As you examine the profiles (Figures 3 and 4), you will note that the T-JTA measures nine bipolar personality traits. The traits measured were selected because they are important components of personal adjustment and because of their influence in interpersonal relationships. The shaded zones on the profile serve as a guide to the evaluation of the scores obtained and as an aid to interpretation. Trait definitions are included at the bottom of each profile to assist the counselor in describing the meaning of specific traits measured.[14]

In addition to its other applications, the T-JTA also has been designed for use in premarital, marital, and family counseling. The test questions have been worded so that a couple may take the test both on themselves and on one another. This is known as a "criss-cross" test.[15] The criss-cross provides a picture of how the couple see each other. How one views a mate is very important in the marriage relationship.

Figure 3 is a profile graph of the T-JTA. Let us suppose that the female in a given couple is above average in dominance, while the male is exceptionally low. If this couple is going to

Figure 3

Taylor-Johnson Temperament Analysis Test

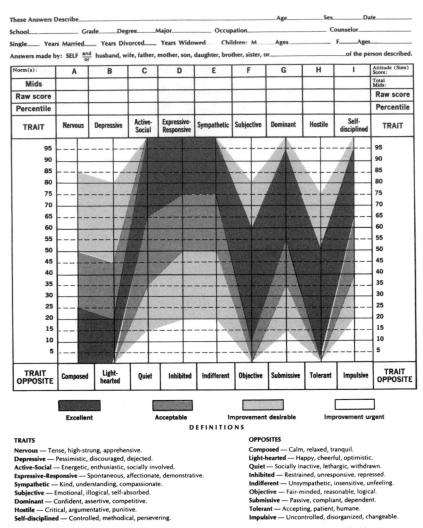

DEFINITIONS

TRAITS

Nervous — Tense, high-strung, apprehensive.
Depressive — Pessimistic, discouraged, dejected.
Active-Social — Energetic, enthusiastic, socially involved.
Expressive-Responsive — Spontaneous, affectionate, demonstrative.
Sympathetic — Kind, understanding, compassionate.
Subjective — Emotional, illogical, self-absorbed.
Dominant — Confident, assertive, competitive.
Hostile — Critical, argumentative, punitive.
Self-disciplined — Controlled, methodical, persevering.

OPPOSITES

Composed — Calm, relaxed, tranquil.
Light-hearted — Happy, cheerful, optimistic.
Quiet — Socially inactive, lethargic, withdrawn.
Inhibited — Restrained, unresponsive, repressed.
Indifferent — Unsympathetic, insensitive, unfeeling.
Objective — Fair-minded, reasonable, logical.
Submissive — Passive, compliant, dependent.
Tolerant — Accepting, patient, humane.
Impulsive — Uncontrolled, disorganized, changeable.

Note: Important decisions should not be made on the basis of this profile without confirmation of these results by other means.

Figure 4

Taylor-Johnson Temperament Analysis Test

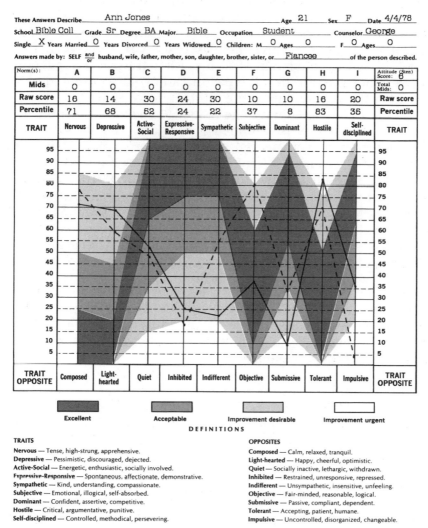

Norm(s):	A	B	C	D	E	F	G	H	I	Attitude (Sten) Score: 6
Mids	O	O	O	O	O	O	O	O	O	Total Mids: O
Raw score	16	14	30	24	30	10	10	16	20	Raw score
Percentile	71	68	62	24	22	37	8	83	36	Percentile
TRAIT	Nervous	Depressive	Active-Social	Expressive-Responsive	Sympathetic	Subjective	Dominant	Hostile	Self-disciplined	TRAIT

These Answers Describe __Ann Jones__ Age __21__ Sex __F__ Date __4/4/78__

School __Bible Coll__ Grade __Sr__ Degree __BA__ Major __Bible__ Occupation __Student__ Counselor __George__

Single __X__ Years Married __O__ Years Divorced __O__ Years Widowed __O__ Children: M __O__ Ages __O__ F __O__ Ages __O__

Answers made by: SELF and/or husband, wife, father, mother, son, daughter, brother, sister, or __Fiancee__ of the person described.

TRAIT OPPOSITE	Composed	Light-hearted	Quiet	Inhibited	Indifferent	Objective	Submissive	Tolerant	Impulsive	TRAIT OPPOSITE

Excellent — Acceptable — Improvement desirable — Improvement urgent

DEFINITIONS

TRAITS

Nervous — Tense, high-strung, apprehensive.
Depressive — Pessimistic, discouraged, dejected.
Active-Social — Energetic, enthusiastic, socially involved.
Expressive-Responsive — Spontaneous, affectionate, demonstrative.
Sympathetic — Kind, understanding, compassionate.
Subjective — Emotional, illogical, self-absorbed.
Dominant — Confident, assertive, competitive.
Hostile — Critical, argumentative, punitive.
Self-disciplined — Controlled, methodical, persevering.

OPPOSITES

Composed — Calm, relaxed, tranquil.
Light-hearted — Happy, cheerful, optimistic.
Quiet — Socially inactive, lethargic, withdrawn.
Inhibited — Restrained, unresponsive, repressed.
Indifferent — Unsympathetic, insensitive, unfeeling.
Objective — Fair-minded, reasonable, logical.
Submissive — Passive, compliant, dependent.
Tolerant — Accepting, patient, humane.
Impulsive — Uncontrolled, disorganized, changeable.

Note: Important decisions should not be made on the basis of this profile without confirmation of these results by other means.

function according to biblical role concepts, some development and adjustment is going to have to take place in both of their lives. If the same female scored high in Subjective, and her prospective mate showed a strong tendency toward being Objective, a potential problem area would exist. For example, she may, and particularly if she also rates high in Impulsive, frequently buy things on the basis of an emotional response. On the other hand, being Objective, he may react with some retaliatory behavior that is consistent with his other traits. By suggesting these various possibilities, the pastor can explore potential problems with the couple during the interpretative session.

I should like to encourage the reader to seek certification. The following case study is intended to demonstrate its value and stimulate interest. Ann scored above average in Depressive and Hostile traits (see Figure 4—solid line represents Ann). When questioned about the degree of hostility, she offered: "It is probably because of my attitude toward my mother." Probing uncovered a tale which, humanly speaking, gave Ann sufficient grounds for her bitterness. It was so disturbing to her that her fiance had to help her tell the story. While empathizing with her, the counselor delineated her responsibility to deal with this bitterness in light of its destructive potential (the Scripture warns of this in Heb. 12:14–15). She responded, "Yes, I must do something about this because it has definitely affected my whole Christian life." She agreed to follow the suggestions outlined to her. At the next session her countenance made it unnecessary to inquire as to the completion of this assignment.

Ann's bitterness had become so intense that it negatively affected relationships with and responses to others. (These findings which surfaced in the interview were confirmed by the low scores in Expressive-Responsive and Sympathetic.) This syndrome in turn depressed Ann, and the depression became the context for further bitterness and hostility. During the T-JTA interpretation the preconditioning problem (a pattern of response to previous life experiences) was surfaced and properly handled. She experienced great hope and quickly began laying aside her other habitually destructive responses. The result was like removing a stuck thermostat from an auto's cooling system. The temperature drops, the red light on the dash goes out, and the engine functions normally. Ann showed a significant decrease in the Depressive and Hostile traits when taking the test a second time at the completion of the counseling.[16]

What actually happens in such cases is that the test results which the counselee himself projects face him objectively with what he is already aware of subjectively. When the counselor probes, the counselee may be motivated to talk about the issue which he believes the test has revealed. If the T-JTA provides only this advantage in some cases, it is well worth the pastor's consideration.

When he has explained the character of the counseling and qualified the couple for continuing the program, the pastor may administer the T-JTA. The test, its purpose, its product, and its use should be carefully declared. This will ease the apprehensiveness that may exist. (Once the counselor is qualified to use the test, he will be able to do this with ease.)

The pastor who does not wish to use the T-JTA may benefit by substitution of the "Trait Factor Inventory." This inventory will also provide the administrator with an understanding of how each mate views the other. He can then develop an interpretative session around this and probe possible trouble areas. He may also wish to use one of the questionnaires in the appendix (pp. 185–192).

Administer the Trait Factor Inventory

The Trait Factor Inventory was developed as an alternative to the T-JTA for those who could not qualify for certification or who chose not to for some reason. This Inventory, however, should not be considered a psychological test. Its only purpose is to provide a relative visual expression of how the couple sees themselves and other significant people in their relationship with regard to these behaviorally expressed personality traits. It in no way suggests the need for psychological treatment. It may suggest the need for Christian counseling to facilitate Christian growth and improved relationships.

Directions for completing the Inventory will be found with the Inventory, at the end of this chapter.

A careful examination of the trait factors on this Inventory will reveal that a number of them are items directly discussed in Scripture. Thus, the pastor-counselor can develop a categorical set of references to discuss with counselees the need and method of improvements that may be indicated.

The counselor would do well to complete a copy of the Inventory and ask his wife to do likewise. He can then graft the responses and discuss them with his wife. This experience will aid him when interacting with counselees.

Administer the Sex Awareness Inventory

Unlike the T-JTA, the Sex Awareness Inventory (SAI) does not require the user to secure credentials to utilize it. He may simply write to the publisher[17] for the test and the accompanying explanatory booklet. Familiarization with this material before administering it is, of course, an indispensable exercise.

Before administering this test to anyone, the pastor-counselor is wise to take it himself. After checking his responses, he can prepare himself for a more efficient use of the test by researching those questions which he missed or those suggested responses with which he finds himself in disagreement. He may also desire to eliminate some questions which he does not consider pertinent to the premarital counseling process.

It is best to instruct the couple not to discuss the test either while they are taking it or until it has been explored in the sessions. If one or the other has difficulty discussing sex, this will forestall a problem until the session where such attitudes themselves can be the subject of investigation.

In the instructions which accompany the test, the administrator is told to have the counselees circle those questions which they would like to discuss when the test is evaluated. However, I have discovered that the questions which need the most clarification are those which the individual misses. This indicates a faulty understanding or a guess, either of which needs correction.

Homework Assignments

Depending on whether or not the pastor-counselor administers the T-JTA and the SAI himself (he may train his secretary to supervise the testing and group several couples together for this purpose), he may actually make the homework assignments before dismissing the couple to take the tests. This is simple procedural matter which each man will have to determine for himself.

The idea of homework assignments may well be the last thing the counselees anticipated as they came for premarital counseling. The purpose should be carefully explained. The purpose is fourfold:

1. The counselees continually give new data as the counselor interacts with the flow of information which frequently stems from the homework. The "halo data"[18] are much more productive, often reflecting attitudes which were expressed while doing the homework.

2. The homework involves the couple in every topic.
3. This approach immerses the prospective mates in the problem-solving process under the guidance of the counselor.
4. Practical projects utilized in conjunction with the interpretation of the T-JTA enable the couple to implement changes that are desirable.[19]

Having delineated the purpose, the counselor's objective is the solicitation of a commitment to perform the assignments. Actually, this is simply a reaffirmation of the commitment made earlier in the session to the homework concept.[20]

Administer the Marriage Attitude Indicator (MAI)

This is a forced choice response form. Each individual must choose a *most* and a *least* answer for each question. For example:

Loving my future partner means:	Most	Least
Giving emotional support	____	____
Thinking/acting in terms of his/her welfare first	____	____
Giving what is desired so that I can get what I desire	____	____
Making him/her feel loved	____	____

When the couple has completed the MAI, the counselor can use one of two strategies. He can ask them to exchange forms, compare responses and discuss them. The better technique is to go through the MAI question by question with them discussing their various answers. This exercise provides fertile ground for expanding their cognitive understanding of the marriage relationship.[21]

Inventory of Reasons for Choosing My Mate [22]

This was the most difficult response form for the counselees in the Field Project to complete. A number of them expressed dismay at having to think objectively about their choice of a mate. It was extremely difficult for them to list specific goals without the use of such phrases as "to honor the Lord in our marriage." This is a valid goal, but unless it is broken down into practical, everyday parts, there is little chance that it will be reached. For example, "We want to honor the Lord in the marriage by learning to solve our differences in a biblical manner and thereby have a daily, harmonious relationship."

The tremendous lack of concrete thinking with respect to this assignment convinced me to include it in the program of premarital counseling. Couples need to be nudged from the shelf of clichés onto the hard floor of reality and learn to articulate in unromantic and tangible language the values they see in their mates and in themselves and the direction in which they are going. If these results are accomplished by this form, its use is justified.

The pastor can enhance his use of this form by a type of role playing. He should think of himself as the counselee and attempt to answer this form completely prior to utilizing it in the counseling process. This exercise will help him guide his counselees into a profitable use of the inventory.

Study and Discuss Together: God-Designed Marriage

All of the couples who participated in the Field Project were Christians. Of these, 67 percent were upper-level Bible college students. When asked if they considered the study of God-Designed Marriage to be redundant because of their church and school experience, 70 percent responded negatively. This illustrates how imperative it is for the premarital counselor to involve the counselees in the study of Scripture regarding the matter of marriage. He should not assume anything about their knowledge. If this is true with respect to the particular class of individuals who participated in the project, how much more so for those who have not been involved in an academic study of the Bible.

This outline with the study guide will provide a scriptural background for a number of the discussions that will develop throughout the program.

Family Worship

Several years ago I was asked to direct a Christmas program in the church in which our family was active. It occurred to me that the program should do more than repeat the Christmas theme. After some consideration, a plan developed which integrated the Christmas theme with family worship. As the spotlight moved across the stage, various approaches to family worship highlighted the Christmas story. At least three men came to me within the next week to indicate that the program had taught them how to conduct family worship. It was something they had wanted to do but simply did not know how to do, and they were too embarrassed to seek help. The pastor can effectively use the premarital counseling program as an opportunity to teach both the necessity and the "how-to" of family worship.

The couple should be asked to commit themselves to two 45-minute periods a week for this purpose. The day and the hour should be agreed on in the first session. Hold the male responsible for calling them together because he is responsible for the spiritual tone in the home. The woman might keep a session log in which she records the Scripture studied, the theme of the passage as they understand it, the observations they make from the passage, and how they decide if what they observed applies to their lives.[23] She could also keep a page to record weekly prayer activity. Record on the left half of the page the prayer requests, and on the right half the answers. Notes reflecting other blessings which they share in these weeks may be added.

Each week the counselor must inquire about their progress and give guidance when it is needed. He will not discuss their log in detail until the sixth session.

Let me urge that the weekly commitment to perform this assignment be a contingency of continuing the program. Seven weeks is long enough to begin a good habit and have it well on the way to becoming an established pattern.

Name _____

Fiancée_____

Reasons for Choosing My Mate

List seven qualities you had in mind that would be desirable in the person you would choose to marry.

1.

2.

3.

4.

5.

6.

7.

List ten reasons which led to your decision to marry your fiancée. (These may include attitudes, personality traits, physical attractiveness, etc.)

1.

2.

3.

4.

5.

6.

7.

8.

9.

10.

List your specific goals for your marriage. These should include more than broad goals such as "To have a marriage that honors the Lord." The idea is to think through the smaller nitty-gritty goals that make such a broad goal possible. (Use back sheet if necessary.)

1.

2.

3.

4.

5.

List at least five contributions that you bring to this marriage that will help make it work (gifts, skills, character traits, experience, etc.)

1.

2.

3.

4.

5.

Outline of God-Designed Marriage

I. Character of God-Designed Marriage
   A. Prepared by God (Gen. 2:18–24; Prov. 2:6–7; Mal. 2:7–17)
   B. Purposes Determined by God (Gen. 1:27–28; 2:18–24)
      1. Companionship (2:18–24)
      2. Sexual Intimacy (2:24)
      3. Children (1:27–28)
   C. Permanence directed by God (Matt. 19:3–19)

II. Functions Within God-Designed Marriage
   A. For the husband (Eph. 5:22–33; 6:4; Col. 3:21; 1 Tim. 5:8)
   B. For the wife (Eph. 5:22–33; 1 Peter 3:1; Prov. 31)
   C. For both (Eph. 5:21)

Study Guide: God-Designed Marriage

I. Prepared by God
   A. List three things you believe the Scripture means in Genesis 2:18. Here are some examples:
      1. The creation was not complete ("not good").
      2. While animals make good friends, man is alone in the world without someone of the opposite sex.
      3. God was not satisfied with only the creation of man. And, he was not satisfied for man to be incomplete.

      (1)

      (2)

      (3)

B. According to Genesis 2:22b, "and brought her unto the man," who initiated the marriage ceremony?

_____

Who was the father of the bride? _____

Who blessed the "wedding"? _____

What implications does this have for your wedding? List them.

C. In Malachi 2:14, marriage is called a "covenant." Look up this word in a dictionary of theology or a Bible dictionary. In light of its definition, draw three practical conclusions about "God-Prepared Marriage." (Here are some suggestions.)
   1. Marriage is not a contract which can be broken if one defaults.
   2. Since God sets the bounds, I am responsible to him to fulfill my responsibilities.
   3. It is necessary for me to work with my mate to solve problems in our relationship.

   (1)

   (2)

   (3)

II. Purposes Determined by God
    A. Companionship
        1. For what reason is Genesis 2:19–20 sandwiched between 2:18 and verses 21 and 22?

        2. Draw five conclusions from the words *alone* and *help meet* in Genesis 2:18 that reflect God's purpose of companionship in marriage.

           (1)

           (2)

(3)

(4)

(5)

3. List the implications you can think of for companionship suggested in Genesis 2:24.

4. In Malachi 2:14, what does the word *thy* which modifies the word *companion* suggest?

B. Sexual intimacy (Gen. 2:24)
   1. As you think of the entire Bible, what is its consistent teaching about the legitimacy of sexual relations?

   What are the bounds? (Heb. 13:4)

   2. In light of 1 Corinthians 7:1–5 (read in a couple of translations), what conclusions can be drawn about the frequency of sexual relations?

   3. In light of the same passage, write out your reaction to sexual response as a duty.

   4. If biblical love is giving, what should be our focus in sexual relations?

   5. List as many reasons as you can think of why sex is not just for procreation.

C. Children (Gen. 1:27–28)

   1. Do you think that every couple should have children, if they can, in light of these verses?

   2. Do you think there is an order of priority here, i.e., companionship, sex, children? If so, for what reasons? If not, for what reasons?

   3. In light of your general knowledge of Scripture, do you think children can make a marriage?

D. Permanence Directed by God (Matt. 19:3–19; 1 Cor. 7:10–16; Rom. 7:1–3; see also Mark 10:1–12; Luke 16:18)

   1. What is God's pleasure regarding marriage?

   2. Does God permit divorce? For what reason?

   3. If divorce takes place, is forgiveness still required of the offended party? Why? Why not?

   4. If divorce takes place as a result of adultery, is reconciliation required?

   5. In light of Ephesians 5:22–32, what is one reason that God desires permanency in marriage?

E. Functions Within God-Designed Marriage
   1. For the husband (Eph. 5:16–6:20; 1 Peter 3:7–9)
     a. The exact verses that speak to the husband are 5:25–32. List the commands that precede this in 5:15–21. How do these affect what is said in 5:25–32? List one implication for each command in 5:15–21.

b. How does Ephesians 6:10–20 affect these husbandly functions? List some implications.

c. Perhaps the most important command is found in 5:18. What does it mean to you to be filled with the Spirit? How will being filled affect your husbandly functions?

d. With privilege comes responsibility. In Ephesians 5:23, God says the husband *is* the head of the wife. List at least five responsibilities that you understand to come with headship.

    (1)

    (2)

    (3)

    (4)

    (5)

e. Give three synonyms for "headship" as you understand it in marriage.

    (1)

    (2)

    (3)

f. Since husbandly headship is to follow the example of Christ over his church, read John 13 and describe how Jesus exercised leadership.

g. List seven ways you can lead your wife after his example.

    (1)

    (2)

    (3)

    (4)

    (5)

    (6)

    (7)

h. Did or does the church deserve the love of Christ?

i. Must your wife be meeting her responsibilities before you love her? (Eph. 5:25).

j. After studying Ephesians 5:26–27, who will God hold responsible to some extent for your wife's development?

k. Check out the words "nourisheth" and cherisheth" in Ephesians 5:29. List five ways in which you can nourish her and five ways of cherishing her.

    (1)   (1)

    (2)   (2)

    (3)   (3)

    (4)   (4)

    (5)   (5)

l. In light of 1 Timothy 5:8, list five ways of managing your home.

    (1)

(2)

(3)

(4)

(5)

2. Functions for the wife.
   a. Read Ephesians 5:22–24. These are the particular verses that speak to the wife's responsibility in the marriage. But note that they are in the context of 5:16–6:20. List the commands given in 5:15–21 and list one implication for each spouse in light of 5:22–24.

   b. Peter speaks to wives in 1 Peter 3:1–6. Please note that Peter uses 2:18 as his example. With this in mind, how would Ephesians 6:10–20 practically affect a wife's lifestyle?

   c. How would you apply 1 Peter 3:1 to a Christian couple?

   d. Define submission (check a dictionary). List five implications of submission for a wife.

   (1)

   (2)

   (3)

   (4)

   (5)

   e. What conclusion would you draw from the example of Christ (John 10:18; 17:4) regarding a wife's inferiority or equality to her husband?

f. Would you say Jesus Christ was a weak/strong person (circle one)? He submitted himself to the will of God (John 13; Phil. 2). What characterized Jesus' life on the earth: joy, ease, delight, comfort, suffering (circle one)? What enabled Jesus to handle his life's lot? Study 1 Peter 2:23 and write out your answer.

g. The wedding vow says "for better, for worse." In light of the previous question, what does this vow mean to you?

h. God clearly teaches that Christians are to be in subjection to the powers that be, but in Acts 4:19 the apostles put the authorities on notice of their determined refusal to submit. What implication does this principle have for wives?

Give three examples when you think a wife would be justified in not submitting to her husband.

(1)

(2)

(3)

3. For both (Eph. 5:21)
   a. For women to answer—
      1. List three ways your husband may be submissive without rendering his leadership invalid.

      (1)

      (2)

      (3)

      2. How is the "headship" which Christ gives him already submissive in character? (Phil. 2:7).

b. For men to answer—
  1. List three examples of submitting to your wife without invalidating your headship.

     (1)

     (2)

     (3)

  2. As a single man you have been independent. How will being submissive to your wife effect change in your lifestyle? List the three most difficult areas for you to deal with.

     (1)

     (2)

     (3)

  3. As a single woman, your wife has had a great deal of freedom. What three habits of her lifestyle will you expect her to change (for example, going shopping alone in the evening)?

     (1)

     (2)

     (3)

Directions for Use of the Trait Factor Inventory

The pastor-counselor should be careful to explain that this is not a psychological test. Its only intent is to provide a visual expression of how the couple sees themselves and other significant people in their relationship with regard to these behaviorally expressed personality traits. It in no way suggests the need for psychological treatment. It may, however, reveal the need for Christian counseling to facilitate Christian growth and improved relationships.

Scoring the inventory involves transposing the letter responses into numerical values. The numerical values are:

$$A = 10$$
$$O = 8$$
$$Y = 6$$
$$R = 4$$
$$B = 2$$
$$T = 1$$

The corresponding numerical value should be placed beside each response on the Inventory. These values may now be placed on the interpretation graph.

The ratings on the graph are separated by two's, with the exception of "T," for the purpose of spreading the graph to enhance its visual value. A point corresponding to the score should be placed in the box representing the proper trait. Graph lines may then be drawn connecting the points. Color coding will make the graph easier to read. A consistent use of the following code is suggested:

Red = Father
Green = Mother
Blue = Male Partner
Orange = Female Partner

The traits are arranged on the graph in two groupings. On the left side of the double line are positive traits, and on the right side are negative traits. This provides the observer with a quick overview. Generally speaking, the higher the numerical values in positive traits the better.

It is important to note "T" responses, which yield a numerical value of one. These responses provide the careful observer with an insight into the relationship of the couple. For example, a "T" response to "easily angered" would raise a question about the depth of communication. Or a "T" response to "rebounds from failure" would raise a question about the honesty or the intimacy of their relationship. If a number of "T's" occur, the counselor should carefully explore how well the couple knows each other, the amount of time they have spent together and under what kinds of circumstances they have been together. (One couple I know had dated one and a half years and were engaged one and a half years. However, he was in the Navy the entire time, and they had been together only on occasional weekends and two weeks in Hawaii on vacation.)

The final two responses on the Inventory are not trait factors. They are important, and provide an opportunity to gain a reading. If there is an "R" or "B" response to these statements, the counselor should explore the reasons and help the individual to structure means of learning to relate more easily with members of his own sex.

If either rates the other "A" or "O" but that individual rates himself "Y", "R", or "B", it is possible that the rater is jealous or feels neglected. Again the counselor should explore these possibilities with the couple.

Please rate the following personality traits of your father (F), mother (M), fiance (W), and yourself (Y). If a parent is dead, rate him (her). If parent died or divorce occurred when you were very young, *do not* rate that person. Rate stepparents or adopted parents as parents.

It is important that you be honest. Think of examples or incidents and respond according to them.

Use the following scale:

A = Usually or regularly
O = Frequently
Y = Occasionally
R = Seldom
B = Never
T = Have not observed

Example:

Trait	**Response**
Takes	F __A__
responsibility	M __Y__
readily	W __O__
	Y __O__

Trait Factor Inventory

Trait

Responsible		Self-Confident	
F __		F __	
M __		M __	
W __		W __	
Y __		Y __	

Dominating

F ___
M ___
W ___
Y ___

Impulsive

F ___
M ___
W ___
Y ___

Irritable

F ___
M ___
W ___
Y ___

Responds too quickly to others

F ___
M ___
W ___
Y ___

Punctual

F ___
M ___
W ___
Y ___

Moody

F ___
M ___
W ___
Y ___

Nervous

F ___
M ___
W ___
Y ___

Jealous

F ___
M ___
W ___
Y ___

Easily hurt

F ___
M ___
W ___
Y ___

Sympathetic

F ___
M ___
W ___
Y ___

Vacillates on decisions

F ___
M ___
W ___
Y ___

Sense of humor

F ___
M ___
W ___
Y ___

Easygoing

F ___
M ___
W ___
Y ___

Sense of duty

F ___
M ___
W ___
Y ___

Easily angered

    F ___
    M ___
    W ___
    Y ___

Selfish

    F ___
    M ___
    W ___
    Y ___

Ambitious

    F ___
    M ___
    W ___
    Y ___

Gossips

    F ___
    M ___
    W ___
    Y ___

Prideful

    F ___
    M ___
    W ___
    Y ___

Responds well to criticism

    F ___
    M ___
    W ___
    Y ___

Merciful

    F ___
    M ___
    W ___
    Y ___

Stubborn

    F ___
    M ___
    W ___
    Y ___

Easily embittered

    F ___
    M ___
    W ___
    Y ___

Impractical

    F ___
    M ___
    W ___
    Y ___

Slanders

    F ___
    M ___
    W ___
    Y ___

Rebounds from failure

    F ___
    M ___
    W ___
    Y ___

Easily depressed

    F ___
    M ___
    W ___
    Y ___

Easily excited

    F ___
    M ___
    W ___
    Y ___

Respectful

    F ___
    M ___
    W ___
    Y ___

Resentful

    F ___
    M ___
    W ___
    Y ___

Self-controlled

    F ___
    M ___
    W ___
    Y ___

Rebellious

    F ___
    M ___
    W ___
    Y ___

Puts others first

    F ___
    M ___
    W ___
    Y ___

Negative attitude

    F ___
    M ___
    W ___
    Y ___

Joins organizations and/or active in groups

    F ___
    M ___
    W ___
    Y ___

Makes friends more easily with same sex

    F ___
    M ___
    W ___
    Y ___

Trait Factor Inventory

1	2	4	6	8	10	Positive
						Responsible
						Responds quickly to others
						Punctual
						Ambitious
						Self-confident
						Sympathetic
						Sense of humor
						Easygoing
						Sense of duty
						Responds well to criticism
						Merciful
						Respectful
						Self-controlled
						Puts others first
						Rebounds from failure

1	2	4	6	8	10	Negative
						Dominating
						Impulsive
						Irritable
						Moody
						Nervous
						Easily angered
						Selfish
						Jealous
						Easily hurt
						Vacillates on decisions
						Stubborn
						Easily embittered
						Impractical
						Gossips
						Prideful
						Resentful
						Rebellious
						Negative attitude
						Slanders
						Easily depressed
						Easily excited
						Joins organizations
						Makes friends more easily with same sex

6

Session Two

Interpret the Taylor-Johnson

As indicated when this test was discussed previously, it is a professional test which requires special training to administer and interpret. The pastor-counselor should study the manual provided with the training and think through the use of biblical data in conjunction with its interpretation.[1]

The interpretation will probably utilize most of this session. The counselor should not hurry. It is important to answer the couple's questions and explain the test carefully. Some people find such a test threatening. Careful, kind, and considerate explanations will enhance the use of the test and put the couple at ease. In some cases it may be necessary to use more than one session for this purpose.

Interpret the Trait Factor Inventory

When graphed, the Inventory will provide a visual projection. There are three possible graphs. The first one records the responses for each of the four persons (father, mother, self, fiance). This provides a comparison of the person responding with each of the other three persons. In discussion with the couple or the individual, the counselor may point out any significant trends or comparisons and explore them. Possible areas of conflict can be suggested and biblical standards and means of changing behavior can be developed as well as how to deal with conflict when it does arise. Each of the other graphs can provide similar opportunities.

A separate graph should be used to plot a criss-cross projection (Male scoring of female partner and female scoring of male partner). This will provide the counselor with a comparison of how the couple sees each other with respect to these trait factors.

The counselor may also develop a couple-comparison by graphing each individual's responses regarding himself on the same graph. This will reflect a comparison of how each sees himself.

Careful note should be taken of the number of "T" responses. A number of such responses indicates that the persons have not really grown to know one another. It may also indicate that they have "fallen in love" and not thought of one another realistically. If "T" occurs frequently with respect to parents, it may reflect a very self-centered person who does not make the effort to know other people. Frequent "T" responses may indicate that a difficult marital adjustment lies ahead.

Since a number of the trait factors are matters directly addressed in Scripture, this Inventory provides ample opportunity to instruct and guide the couple. Each counselor would do well to go through the Scripture and list specific verses to which he may refer or suggest as a Bible study for homework assignments.

Discussion of this Inventory and the study guide (God-Designed Marriage), which the couple should have completed for this session, will occupy the entire session. As much time as is needed should be given to each. Discussion to the satisfaction of the couple as well as the counselor should be the goal.

Discuss God-Designed Marriage

The Socratic method is the best way to handle the discussion of this outline. Move through the outline point by point. Ask the couple to express their understanding of each point. Explore their answers. Ask them to restate them in other words. Question conclusions they draw. Seek to have them defend each concept they verbalize. Do not be satisfied with generalizations or evangelical clichés. Be sure they draw out the practical implications of the biblical teachings. What, for example, in behavioral terms, does it mean for the husband to treat his wife "as the weaker vessel"? If they understand what God is saying, they can articulate it in their own words.

Do not take this assignment for granted. It is important. Even those young people who have been the spiritual leaders in the church or who have attended a Christian college may not grasp these truths in a practical manner. A young man who was looked up to as a dynamic spiritual leader on the Christian college campus which I attended has made a disaster of his marriage simply because he did not understand the application of these Bible basics to his family life. This outline focuses on the primary teaching of God about marriage. From an understanding of the truth considered in this homework assignment grows the practical implications discussed in the remainder of this program.

The pastor-counselor can prepare himself for a beneficial conference by working through the study guide and developing a set of questions which can serve as his guide for this topic.

Homework Assignments

Comparison of Role Concepts Inventory [2]

As a counseling tool, this Inventory is valuable. Its main use is that of a handout for homework. The couple should be asked to complete it separately. They should be informed that a number of the items will seem vague and contingent on circumstances. They should discuss their differing responses. In most instances agreement will be reached through realizing how they interpreted each concept. Caution them not to argue about their differences, but as they discuss their opposing opinions to place a check beside those about which they seem to have unresolved conflict.

Read Chapter 3 in **Christian Living in the Home** *by Adams, and do the worksheet on problem solving*

This assignment is obviously designed as a frontal attack on the matter of problem solving. The following principles may be suggested to the couple along with the illustrations to help them profit from this exercise.

1. *Define the problem*—We are going further in our intimacy than we should.
2. *Determine if Scripture deals directly with this problem*—If intimacy has reached the stage of premarital sex, the Scripture clearly forbids this practice.
3. *Determine what implications or principles of Scripture can solve this problem*—With reference to the issue suggested in number one, the Word says: (a) He who lusts has already com-

mitted adultery—What can one do but lust in the midst of
heavy petting? (Matt. 5:27–28). (b) Think on pure things
(Phil. 4:6–9). (c) Flee youthful lusts (2 Tim. 2:22).

4. *Determine practical means for implementing biblical
   directives*—For example, in relation to the problem of sexual intimacy, the couple may agree to: (a) Limit their time
   alone in private situations; (b) Not to become irritated or
   offended if either asks the other to refrain from physical
   affection (or a particular type of physical affection); (c)
   Occupy their time together in Christian service or other
   wholesome activity, etc.

5. *Determine impediments to solving any given problem,
   record them, and bring them to the next session*—"He simply refused to consider the possibility of limiting our private time."

The particular problem cited above as an example for the application of problem-solving techniques was chosen because it is a
problem faced by every young couple to some extent. It is a very
practical consideration as LeMasters found in his research. He
concluded that sex (both intercourse and petting) before marriage
may overshadow serious differences between couples, with the
result that they do not become evident until after the marriage.[3]

Learning how to make decisions and settle issues is vitally
important for many reasons within the marriage relationship,
but McGinnis summarized it well when he wrote:

> Some people think that because they love each other, they will be
> able to reach decisions well. This is not so. Love *results* from sat-
> isfactory decision-making; it does not cause it.[4]

Pastor, teach problem solving! Press for thorough completion
of this assignment.

Write a paragraph on how 1 Corinthians 13:4–8 applies to daily living as a couple

This facet of the program is calculated to reach two objectives. It is hoped that it will engage each of the individuals in
sifting for him/herself the implications of true biblical love.
And, secondly, it is designed to lay a groundwork for the discussion of the character of love in the next session.[5]

As the counselor, the pastor should emphasize that he is
expecting this paragraph to be concrete. To illustrate, he might
read these verses and ask, "How is love not rude?" He may then

Worksheet on Problem Solving

Name _____ Fiancée_____

List below the solutions to at least three problems that you have solved together God's way. These should be problems where you have had differences of opinion, difficult decisions to make, arguments, or personal antagonisms to overcome. If you have some current problems, list them and record solutions and how these solutions were reached. (Adapted from Adams' *Christian Living in the Home*, p. 68.)

Define Problem	Determine Scripture	Determine Implications	Determine Implementation	Determine Impediments

continue, "Well, suppose that you, Joe, have a habit of cracking your knuckles at will—though, of course, you have been polite and not done this in Jane's presence during your courtship. Now, however, that you are married, you relax and continue your practice at home. If Jane finds this offensive, it will be rude of you to continue it. Love will curtail this habit." An illustration of this nature will help insure that they understand "concrete" in terms of this assignment.

Name _____

Fiancée_____

Comparison of Role Concepts Inventory*

Check the appropriate column
Agree / Disagree / Not Sure

____ ____ ____ To say "nothing" when asked by your mate if there is something wrong is better than starting an argument.

____ ____ ____ "Fighting" is always wrong between mates.

____ ____ ____ The Bible teaches that a wife must always obey her husband.

____ ____ ____ It is the husband's role to determine the responsibilities of each mate.

____ ____ ____ Strict discipline will produce well-behaved and well-developed children.

____ ____ ____ Fathers should be disciplinarians.

____ ____ ____ The man should be head of the home.

____ ____ ____ The wife's earnings are her personal funds.

____ ____ ____ It is a wife's responsibility to have a house neat and clean at all times.

____ ____ ____ Since the wife is a responder, only the husband should initiate lovemaking.

____ ____ ____ The husband should plan the budget and manage the money.

____ ____ ____ A man should have one night out with the boys each week.

____ ____ ____ Cooking is a wife's responsibility.

____ ____ ____ A wife is as responsible for child discipline as a husband.

____ ____ ____ The yard, painting, and maintenance are the husband's responsibility.

____ ____ ____ A limit on spending by each mate without consulting the other should be agreed on.

____ ____ ____ Leisure time and recreation should be spent together.

____ ____ ____ To argue is human: therefore, arguing is part of marriage.

____ ____ ____ It is the responsibility of the wife to teach values to the children.

____ ____ ____ A wife should not work outside the home.

____ ____ ____ A husband should not be expected to wash dishes, scrub floors, etc.

____ ____ ____ Since a wife has more time with children, she has greater responsibility for them.

____ ____ ____ When a wife has been blessed with a special talent, she should have a career to utilize it.

____ ____ ____ The Bible teaches that men are responsible for their jobs and women are responsible for home and children.

_____ _____ _____   A joint checking account is the best way to handle money.

_____ _____ _____   Marriage is a: 50% - 50% proposition.

_____ _____ _____   60% - 40% proposition.

_____ _____ _____   100% - 100% proposition.

_____ _____ _____   If a husband and wife have an impasse on a major decision, the husband should take responsibility for the decision and make it according to his thinking.

_____ _____ _____   Husbands should baby-sit so wives can go out with their friends.

_____ _____ _____   It is a true saying, "Women are more emotional than men."

_____ _____ _____   Children can play a part in family decision making as they grow up.

_____ _____ _____   If the husband fails to take leadership, a wife must take over.

_____ _____ _____   Sometimes a wife must use her children as leverage to move her husband.

_____ _____ _____   A woman can mold her husband the way she wants him after they are married.

_____ _____ _____   Since a husband earns the major portion of the family income, he should be more free to spend money on sports, cars, etc.

_____ _____ _____   Using sex as a bargaining tool is sometimes necessary when a mate does not respond to requests.

_____ _____ _____   The authority given to men in the home by God makes him the "general" and his wife the enlisted person who must take orders.

——— ——— ——— A woman should conform to her husband's preference of hair length, dress style, etc.

——— ——— ——— Planning a vacation is a husband's task. Plans need not be discussed with wife.

——— ——— ——— A woman should be in charge of decorating a home.

——— ——— ——— It is a husband's privilege to determine social engagements.

——— ——— ——— A wife should have total responsibility for purchasing children's clothing.

*This inventory is a revision and development of "The Role Comparison Concepts" and is used by permission. James R. Hine, *Your Marriage Analysis and Renewal* (Danville, Ill.: Interstate Publishers and Printers).

7

Session Three

Discuss Communication

McGinnis says, in the introductory chapter to his book:

> The book frequently demonstrates that differences in expecta-
> tions, methods of communication and patterns of decision-making
> [problem-solving] underlie most of the conflicts between hus-
> bands and wives.[1]

I would agree. But communication is the most important. Our
expectations of one another can be modified through communication, and problem-solving cannot function without communication. Everything in this program is geared to deal with these
three broad areas in terms of specifics. The Christian counselor
must be careful to instruct every couple thoroughly in the four
basic biblical rules of communication to insure the greatest benefit from the remainder of the program and the continuing application of its many facets to their daily lives.[2]

The most compact passage of Scripture with respect to communication is Ephesians 4:25–32. There are four basic rules in
this passage that govern communication. These might be called
"Four Laws of Communication" or "God's Rules for Fair Fighting."
A colleague, ministering to a gathering of pastors and their

wives from this passage, entitled his message, "How to Fight with Your Wife."[3]

The pastor-counselor should go through this passage with the couple, developing some of the following thoughts.

Rule No. 1—Stop lying and start telling truth (v. 25). Most young sincere Christian couples will look at the counselor with a note of disbelief when he suggests this first rule. "Now I know that you do not think of yourselves as lying to each other," he might interject, "but let me illustrate that Christians do at times lie to each other. Consider Tom and Joann."

Tom and Joann declared that their marriage was finished. They had come for counseling as a last-ditch effort. As the case began to unravel, it became apparent that their troubles had started early in the marriage. Pressing the issue of their early relationship uncovered a pattern of not kissing good night. When questioned about the reasons for this unusual practice, Tom said that Joann frequently gave him the silent treatment in bed. He indicated that when he had inquired about what was wrong she gave him the cool response, "Nothing." Finally, Joann began to cry. Through her tears she sobbed, "You never appreciated the things I did right from the very beginning. All you were interested in was my body!" Tom responded to this with a look of disbelief.

"What things in particular did he not appreciate?" the pastor asked.

Further discussion revealed that Tom would crawl under the covers and mumble something about the way the bed had been made. This hurt Joann's feelings, because she wanted so much to please him. She would get quiet. Dismayed and frustrated, Tom would seek to find out what was bothering her. Being afraid of a fight, Joann would lie by replying, "Nothing."

This sequence occurred frequently. Sometimes Tom would press her about her quietness, and her reply, "Nothing is wrong, but there will be if you don't stop asking me," only intensified her lie.

Unquestionably, Tom should have told Joann that having the sheets tucked in made him uncomfortable. But he did not want to hurt her by finding fault with her work. He hoped that she would get the idea and change the method of making the bed. However, Joann should not have lied when questioned by Tom as to what was bothering her. A simple statement like, "Honey, I want to please you. If I am doing something displeasing, please tell me what it is so that I can correct it," would most likely have cleared the air without a fight. Lying almost destroyed the marriage.

People can identify with an illustration of this nature. Another couple in my counseling office was experiencing sexual problems. They assured me that they did not have a communication or relational problem. After two sessions of fruitless work, I began going over this passage with them. I shared the illustration above when they indicated that they were not guilty of lying to each other. In the midst of the illustration, when sharing Joann's answer of "nothing" to the question, "What is bothering you?" the husband said, "Yes, that's what this one does."

Christians will lie to each other. They will lie to protect their relationship from the stress that they believe will result from a confrontation. Couples must be cautioned against this practice.

Rule No. 2—Keep current (vv. 26–27). In the example of Tom and Joann, matters were compounded because they broke this rule also. God clearly says that going to bed angry with each other is a sure way to allow the devil to drive a wedge into the relationship. Anger not dealt with is anger saved for future use. Joann's anger had turned into bitterness and became generalized from the specific problem to the whole marriage. God's rule is plain. Be sure that anger is laid aside before retiring. It is possible that the problem which caused the anger cannot be solved that quickly. However, the anger can be put to rest by agreeing to settle the issue at a time and place that is satisfactory to both individuals. The relationship can be reestablished even though the issue cannot be immediately settled. Or, perhaps confession and reconciliation are needful. Since initiating reconciliation is the responsibility of both the offended and the offender, neither can use a ruptured relationship as an excuse "to let . . . the sun go down upon your wrath."[4]

Rule No. 3—Assault the issue, not your mate (vv. 29–30). The word translated "corrupt communication" in the King James Version may well be rendered "cutting or slicing remarks" in contemporary language. This is contrasted by the apostle to the kind of speaking that should be characteristic of the new person in Christ. We should speak that which tends to build others, i.e., things which strengthen their Christian character (even criticism can be offered in this way) in any given situation (literally, "toward improvement of the need").

Amos' verbal assault on Mary illustrates how this kind of behavior becomes habitual and stifles communication. They had been married five years. He was a well-established farmer in his fifties when he married Mary, who was a divorcee. Their five years of marriage had been a history of separation and reconciliation. As we discussed an incident concerning finances, a constant problem, Amos said, "Well now, no one knew about my buying that property but my daughter, myself, and you. Yet, now the whole area knows about it, and they found out from Mrs. Cox, to whom you are always crying the blues. So, you must have been shooting off your mouth again!"

"I didn't tell her," Mary replied sharply, "and you can take your money and burn it for all I care!"

The writer of Proverbs (18:6) says, "A fool's lips enter into contention, and his mouth calleth for strokes." One cutting remark elicits another. Communication ceases, and character defamation often develops, destroying respect and love. Little wonder that the injunction not to grieve the Holy Spirit is given between this rule and the next. The Christian's use of his or her mouth directly affects the person of the Holy Spirit.

Rule No. 4—Pro-act, don't react (vv. 31–32). All those things listed in verse 31 are reactionary. They are retaliatory. They destroy communication. They force defensiveness because they directly attack the other person whereas the instruction of verse 32 is what may be called "pro-acting," acting toward the other person. It is being understanding of the other person's frustrations. It is listening to another viewpoint. It is gently considering another's feelings. It is letting love cover a multitude of sins. In short, it is acting in the very practical matter of daily living as God has acted toward us through Christ (v. 32).

Take the very real problem of some women who become edgy just before their regular menstrual cycle. The husband who is pro-acting will say, "Honey, let me know when it is that time. I'll make every effort to keep things on an even keel for those two or three days and will try not to be out of town, so I can help with the children as much as possible."

Much more detail could be developed about communication. However, a pastor who will share this passage with a couple as we have done above can aid them in building a biblical frame of reference for communication. He should be alert for indications that they have already experienced difficulty in one or more of these troublesome areas and probe the problem. Nothing illustrates a principle better than learning how to apply it to one's own experience.

It is unnecessary to develop all the various psychological reasons for not communicating. If the couple will learn to practice the biblical behavior suggested in this passage, they will be dealing with the psychological.

If the counselor deems further instruction to be warranted, he might assign the reading of Wright's book, *Communication: Key to Your Marriage,* and provide a worksheet for homework.[5]

Discuss Role Concepts

This can be a very simple process. The couple should be asked to specify items on the Role Concepts Comparison sheet on which they found varying opinions. Asking them to share how they discussed these differences and whether or not they came to an agreement will give the pastor one more insight into the problem-solving ability of the couple. If they found some statements about which they did not arrive at a satisfactory conclusion, the counselor should discuss these and suggest biblical principles that can help in the resolution of their differences.

Because of its simplicity, the relevancy of this assignment and its in-session consideration should not be overlooked. One couple in my research project, for example, experienced a number of problems as a result of dissimilar opinions about roles. The biblical concepts are challenged in our society. Young people cannot escape this influence.[6]

Discuss the Character of Love

The value of this discussion is reflected by Small when he writes:

> Robert Moore describes this transition vividly, saying that communication in courtship is easy for it merely extends romantic illusions. Romanticizing, the young man comes out with something like, "She's so much fun to be with and talk to. She's so keenly interested in everything I do. Life with her will be great!" The young woman will likely come out with, "This is my kind of guy. He's so neat, so considerate, and so interested in me. He pays attention to everything about me."[7]

The task of "deromanticizing" love was begun by asking the counselees to write the paragraph on 1 Corinthians 13. This should provide opportunity to emphasize that *love* is *giving, not getting;* that love demands work to grow. Beginning with the comments they wrote, the pastor can embark on the exploration of the character of love with them. The inadequate understanding on the part of many should not be surprising. Many young people have grown up in homes where there was little true love. Even many Christian homes fail miserably as learning models for the fledgling.[8] Young people are constantly bombarded with Hollywood concepts and may have been living unrestrained lives which have been dependent on emotional infatuation and/or sexual appeal. Love is not a feeling first. It is not an experience first. They must learn that love is basically something they make happen and not something that just happens.

God does not ask the Christian to love his neighbor. He commands him to do so. If God commands us, he has made us capable of loving our neighbor. The fact that God commands love demonstrates that it is a volitional matter. In marriage, one's closest neighbor is a mate. The philosophical distinctions of the various Greek words for love are not important to this discussion. What is pertinent is the functional definition. How does the love that God speaks of behave? What does and/or will it do?

After discussing their paragraphs, commenting and expanding as they give occasion, I usually turn rather abruptly toward the woman and present the following situation. "Let's say you have agreed to save 50 percent of your combined salaries for the first three years of your marriage as a down payment on a home. At the end of the first year, he comes home one night and is very quiet. When you ask what is bothering him, he replies, 'Well, Honey, you know that I've always had a desire to have a Porsche. And, well, I've been thinking about that $8,000 we have in the bank. That money could make it possible for me to buy a new 914, and the payments wouldn't be any more than our car payments have been this year. I think tomorrow I'm going to the bank, withdraw that money, and buy that Porsche I looked at today.' If after you make every reasonable effort to persuade him otherwise, he still goes out and buys that car, will you support him as your husband? Will you enjoy the car with him? Will you be long-suffering and not become angered? In short, will your behavior continue to be loving?"

Or, to think in terms of the male partner, I might ask, "Jim, if ten years from now Mary drifts from the Lord, becomes seventy-five pounds overweight, sloppy and foul-mouthed, will you continue to protect, to trust, to hope, and to persevere with her?"

On more than one occasion, I have had couples thank me later in the counseling for pressing this issue via illustrations.

One other matter that merits elucidation before leaving the subject of love is the fact that in the marital relationship only the husband is commanded to love (though the older women are commanded to teach the younger women how to love their husbands). Small writes penetratingly when he says:

Ephesians 5:25–33 is addressed to husbands, and forms a singularly complete word to husbands in New Testament instruction. . . . [It] provides the key to understanding the spiritual dynamics of Christian married love.

The husband is to take the initiative in love; he is made responsible for married love. He is the lover. The command is: "Husbands, love your wives." [This is not to say that the wife cannot initiate sexual relations according to 1 Cor. 7]. One will seek in vain to find such a command for wives! It never says, "Wives, love your husbands." Some would suppose that this is unnecessary because husbands are such lovable fellows anyway! But hardly! Rather, the whole mystery of creative and reciprocal love is embodied in this principle. It is the logical counterpart in marriage to the love relation between Christ and the believer. It is love creating its own response. In loving his wife, the husband causes her to love him in return.[9]

In other words, love begets love. Since the husband is placed at the head of the wife, he is made responsible to be the catalyst of marital love.

Homework Assignments

List any problem you have had with prospective in-laws

It is important to encourage the counselees to list even such things as insignificant "friendly" arguments over political issues, the best restaurants, or which fishing gear is proper equipment to use on their favorite lake. This material can provide an excellent opportunity to share instruction regarding in-law relationships later.

Work out a proposed budget

To give the couple some guidance, the counselor may duplicate the suggested worksheet included with the homework materials at the end of the chapter. This assignment is extremely important. Many couples simply have no idea of how much money it will take to operate a home. One girl in my research group indicated that she believed $200 per month would be sufficient. Unfortunately, too many parents have not taught their children how to manage money. Frequently they have lived off mother's and dad's charge cards and have not been held responsible for their expenses. This assignment can help the pastor be sure they understand the Christian principles of money management from the beginning.

If the couple does not know how much their income will be, a community average can be used for the purpose of completing the budget exercise. Another good source for a projected income is that of a teacher's starting salary in your community.

The couple should be encouraged to investigate the items on the budget. This can be accomplished by actually looking at apartments, talking with insurance representatives, and interviewing their parents or other Christian couples.

Discuss children

The counselees should be asked to consider three subjects. First, the number of children they desire. Secondly, the approach to discipline which they will employ. Thirdly, their attitude toward children in relation to material possessions. They should agree to the relative value of things in relationship to the suppression of natural child behavior. In other words, they should think through which is more important, immaculately maintained possessions or a happy, wholesome atmosphere in which children learn proper respect for things.

Name _____

Fiancée_____

A Budget for the First Year of Marriage

Flexible Expenses

Furniture, household equipment/repairs   _____
Medical and dental care   _____
Clothing   _____
Vacation and travel   _____
Education   _____
Entertainment/recreation/hobbies   _____
Christmas and other gifts   _____

LIVING EXPENSES

Food and household supplies   _____
Personal supplies (haircuts, toiletries, etc.) _____
Cleaning and laundry   _____
Papers/magazines/etc.   _____

TRANSPORTATION

Auto purchase (monthly payment)   _____
Auto operation   _____
Public transportation   _____
Total _____ ÷ 12 = _____ per month

Fixed Expenses

Tithes and offerings _____
(regular, faith promise, or special) _____
Housing (rent or mortgage) _____
Professional or union dues _____
Organizational membership(s) _____
Professional journals _____
Vehicle licenses _____

TAXES
Property _____
Head and/or wage _____
School _____
Other assessments _____

UTILITIES
Heat _____
Electric _____
Phone _____
Water _____
Sewer _____

INSURANCE
Auto _____
Life _____
Health _____
Homeowners, renters _____
Other _____

INSTALLMENT PAYMENTS
Loans (other than auto) _____
Department stores _____
Other _____
Savings
Total _____ ÷ 12 = _____ per month
    Total proposed income $_____ (net, not gross)
    Total proposed expenses $_____
        Black $_____
        Red $_____

Name _____

Fiancée_____

Communication: Key to Your Marriage

Directions: Read chapters 3, 4, 5, 9 of *Communication: Key to Your Marriage* by H. Norman Wright and answer these questions independently. You may discuss them after each of you have written your answers.

1. "Listen more, talk less" for effective communication, concludes Wright. Explain his reasoning.
2. Before you read the book, define listening. After reading the book, write out Wright's definition. Compare this with your definition. Now list three ways you can improve your listening.
3. Do you find it difficult to concentrate (without being distracted easily) when your fiance is speaking to you? Give three brief reasons. Develop three practical ways to help you concentrate.
4. Are you interested in facts or the sense (communicated with gestures, facial expressions, etc.) of his or her conversation? For the next five days take notes on your conversations. Give special attention to what you learned from gestures, facial expressions, etc.
5. Do you automatically "tune out" or jump to conclusions when your fiance uses certain words or phrases? If so, list them. Discuss these with your fiance and find out (write down) what they mean to him (her).
6. When communication is frustrating, do you work with your fiance toward understanding or do you "let it go"? Give an example.
7. Do you ever pretend attentiveness? If so, list those things that dull your interest. List some things you can do to cultivate interest in your fiance's interests.
8. On page 66, Wright suggests some reasons for the lack of communication. Read these. Do any of them correspond to what you have listed to any of the above questions? If so, which ones? For each one you list, suggest a positive course of action you can take to correct the problem.

8

Session Four

Discuss Budget and Approach to Money

The family financial structure is potentially inflammatory. The use and abuse of money, the variation of cultural values, and differences in family economic levels may each produce conflict. Money may also become the focus of other unresolved problems. If the counselor is able to guide the couple into a biblical philosophy of financial management and teach them how to implement these principles, he will render a service that will glorify God and benefit both the couple and the church of Jesus Christ.

Beginning with an explanation of 1 Timothy 3:4, the pastor-counselor can clarify the concept of a man *ruling well* his own household. The word in the original is literally "to superintend." A good rendering would be: "He must manage well his own family." Many men have the idea that to be the man of the house they have to handle the finances. This is not true. They may very well delegate the day-to-day operations to their wives. Delegation does not mean dereliction. If the husband goes through money like a child through a box of popsicles and his wife has been blessed with wisdom and restraint, the wife should handle the finances. Whatever the situation with an individual couple, they should be encouraged to agree on a policy.

115

I have frequently suggested to couples that during the first year of their marriage they would be wise to agree on some *ground rules* regarding personal expenditures. Depending on their projected income, the suggestion has been made that they do not spend more than $20 without discussing the expenditure with their partner, and not more than $50 on each other's Christmas presents or $25 for birthdays.

Credit is another matter that needs clarification. Some couples rather naively decide that they will not buy on credit with the exception of a house or car. Others are so accustomed to credit cards (which Dad has heretofore supported) that credit has become a way of life. Both extremes should be avoided. In our present society, a good credit rating is imperative. The following guidelines will help a couple establish good credit:

1. Establish a credit card account with a major department store and ask that a $500 limit be placed on it.
2. Establish a credit card account with a major oil company. For the first six months put cash in an envelope each time the card is used, to insure the ability to pay the full amount at billing date. After this initial period, an accurate amount can be budgeted to cover the bill.
3. Establish credit with a pharmacy. This will provide a means for securing emergency drug supplies if cash is not available.[1] This also provides an accurate accounting of drug expenditures for income tax purposes.
4. Establish a checking account at a local bank.
5. Establish a savings account at the same bank.
6. Sometime during the first year borrow $1000 from this bank. Open a savings account at another bank and deposit this $1000. Each month withdraw the amount needed to repay the loan payment. This will cost a few dollars in interest, but it will help to establish a line of credit at the bank. The second savings account may be maintained by alternating monthly savings deposits between the two banks. The couple must be impressed with the importance of paying these accounts on time.
7. Last, but perhaps most importantly for a Christian couple, limit indebtedness to the value of your assets. Don't borrow beyond the value of assets you are willing to dispose of to settle your accounts.

Furniture and household appliances are good projects to save toward and purchase with cash unless there is an emergency situation. (Garage sales, some appliance stores, and major outlet stores often yield good savings for little sacrifice of quality on both new and used appliances.)[2]

Helping the couple keep Christ in Christmas can be accomplished by aiding them in keeping frustration and anger out of Christmas. January is a month known for depression. I have often wondered if this is not related to the "month-after blues" induced by bill paying and guilt over disregarding the strong resolutions to control Christmas spending. A couple in a church I served taught me a workable solution to this problem which can be utilized by any couple. Joe and Jane, having experienced the "month-after blues," decided on a plan of action. Each year during the last two weeks of November they sit down together and determine who will be on that year's Christmas list. Then they determine how much they can afford to budget for that Christmas. Next, they put in order of priority in terms of expenditure the names on their list. Using a good quality mail order catalog and considering children's requests, they begin to match potential presents with the allotted budget for each person. When they have agreed on *every* item, they proceed with purchases. Perhaps what another couple in our acquaintance does could be added to this idea. They take a day to go shopping together for the Christmas presents. We have tried it. If well planned, it makes an enjoyable day.

What forms the crux of the illustration above is communication, discussion, and agreement concerning expenditures. The prospective mates must understand that these are the functional components of sound family financial planning.

Responsibility to provide for one's family (1 Tim. 5:8) and the support of the work of the Lord (2 Cor. 9) should be clearly grasped.[3] A good suggestion to the couple which will facilitate the fulfillment of both of these obligations is the 10-10-10-70 budget. Ten percent is put aside for the Lord, 10 percent is earmarked for regular savings, 10 percent builds a contingency fund, and 70 percent provides a cost-of-living budget.[4] If both partners plan to work for the first few years, this budget may be applied to his salary, while her entire income may be placed in a special high-interest account after subtracting at least a tithe. To learn the grace of giving, such couples should be urged to consider more than a tithe.

Discuss Insurance and Investments

Some will ask, "What is a pastor-counselor doing talking about insurance and investments?" The answer is simple. Experience has shown that many couples do not have the slightest idea of the importance of insurance and investments. Therefore, it seems that good premarital counseling must at least suggest types of insurance to be considered, approximate minimums of coverage, and a few safe investments.

Health insurance

Not to have health insurance in today's market can mean sheer financial disaster. A couple of our acquaintance who did not have insurance coverage incurred some emergency medical expenses ten years ago. They are still paying on these bills. Such circumstances which put unnecessary burdens on families can be avoided by carrying adequate medical insurance. For those entering the Christian ministry, this can be a particularly thorny problem to which they should be alerted. If they must provide their own health insurance, the couple should be encouraged to investigate at least two companies to compare prices and coverage. It is also wise to advise them to determine if they are eligible for a group policy through some organization to which they belong or can join.

Life insurance

Every couple will have to decide the minimum coverage for their family. I have offered the following guidelines to couples.

Husband—$150,000. This will bury him and provide minimal living expenses for his wife from investment of the principle. The policy may be retirement income in nature. Beyond this, he can add term insurance. This same type policy should be used to cover any indebtedness incurred. It is also wise to carry mortgage insurance.

Wife—$25,000. This will provide a funeral and pay child care for a limited time. The policy should also be retirement in nature. If there is more than one child it may be wise to carry $100,000 to insure child care.

Children—$5,000 each. Again, this will cover a moderate funeral.

Homeowners or renters insurance

These policies cover liability and contents of dwelling against fire, theft, and so on. Encourage the couple to investigate this type policy with a good insurance agent as soon as they rent or buy.

Package insurance

Companies today offer insurance packages that include such diverse items as homeowners and automobiles. There are also package life insurance policies which cover the entire, even expanding, family.

Investments

A couple can be advised that a high-interest bank certificate is the safest high-yield investment. Beyond this, recommend that they read about investments and seek a reliable investment advisor before involving any sizable amount of funds.

The above material could be printed and handed to each couple for consideration, but this would short-circuit the process. They need one person whom they can trust to speak with them face to face regarding these matters. The "halo data" may suggest a problem for the agenda to be discussed before leaving the topic of money. In some cases this material can be covered quickly. Knowledge about the individual couple will dictate the course of this session. Opportunity to provide adequate guidance for the couple should not be missed.

An excellent guide for Christian family financial management has been prepared by the Louis Niebauer Company.[5] Every premarital counselor would do well to consider giving a copy to the counselees.[6]

Wills

A will is an important legal instrument even for the newlyweds. Suppose a couple were married only six months and the remaining parent of one mate died, making them heirs of $100,000. Then two weeks later they were both killed in an auto accident. What would happen to these funds? Would there be good stewardship of them? No! But a will would provide for their expenditure according to the couple's desires.

It is also important to have a will specifying arrangements for children. For example, we have appointed my best friend and his wife as guardians for our children. They are Christians, are compatible in age, and have children of similar ages. Our funds would go into trust for the care and education of the children. If no will is provided, the state may well determine the children's future.

You may consider developing a resource booklet for these young people. This booklet could include doctors, lawyers, insurance representatives, real estate representatives, and other helpful information and individuals you can recommend.

Discuss Children

In the homework assigned last session, family planning, infertility, and adoption were not suggested for discussion by the couple. The pastor-counselor can begin the topic of children by investigating attitudes in these areas. These are questions about which he might learn more from the "halo data" than from a report on homework assignments.

Family planning depends on birth control. A couple may determine that three children three years apart would be just fine, without considering the ease and regularity with which the wife may become pregnant. Or, one of the couple might assume the use of birth control because they are talking about the number and spacing of children, while the other has convictions restraining participation.

Jack and Jane are a good example. When the subject of family planning via birth control was mentioned, he responded, "I think those matters should be left to the Lord." The slow roll of Jane's eyes indicated that she did not agree.

"Jane," the counselor questions, "you do not agree, do you?"

"No, I'm sure that both of us are going to want to enjoy our sexual relationship, and I don't want to have all the children his mother has had. With fear of pregnancy always with me, I'm afraid it will take the joy out of the relationship."

A lively discussion ensued. The counselor had opportunity to help Jack explore his thinking in terms of the Scriptures.[7] He and Jane had been aware of the differences in their opinions before, but politely avoided the subject for fear of fighting.

Infertility is a problem that few couples consider before it is a problem. The discussion of this potential problem provides an opportunity to determine if their companionship has priority. Some couples' main justification for marriage is the bearing of children. But once married, they will have to live together, even if they cannot bear children. Attitudes about this possibility should be explored.

Provided that children are not a disproportionate motivation for marrying and infertility becomes a reality, would adoption be considered an option? Here again, the couple may have completely divergent views and in some cases be totally unaware of it. When the possibility of adoption is proposed, their concepts will be surfaced and may be aired. "Halo data" may again reveal the true emotional responses of one or the other, even though each gives a verbal consent to the idea of adoption. If so, probing will force the couple to verbalize true thinking. It can then be dealt with by both parties. Not desiring adoption, if bearing one's own children is not possible, is not in itself wrong. What is important is that both agree or are willing to accept the other's viewpoint.

Attention should be given to the homework prepared on the subject of children. The couple had been asked to discuss three matters: number of children, approach to discipline, and attitude in relation to material possessions.

The discussion of the number of children is usually not a great problem unless there is a divergence in the number desired or the wife-to-be is highly career-oriented and desires no children, while her mate does. In these situations, extended counseling may be necessary.

Even in Christian circles, the approach to discipline can vary considerably. By the work the couple has done the counselor can determine two things: (1) Do these young people have a grasp of the biblical teaching of child rearing? (2) Are they generally in basic agreement? The instruction should be commensurate with their need.

The counselor should ask questions like: (1) What do you think when visiting in a friend's home and three or four neighbor children clamor into the kitchen with the children of the house? (2) How does it affect you to see the arms of a chair worn through? (3) What do you think about the folks who live in a home where there are fingerprints on the walls? These kinds of questions can help you determine the attitudes of the couple toward material possessions in terms of children in the home. What I am suggesting is that the counselor be concerned with the existing attitudes and be of assistance to one or both of the counselees in learning to adjust attitudes where necessary. They need to recognize that children are full of energy, usually not deliberately destructive, and grow up better adjusted in a home that is balanced between teaching proper respect of things and freedom to develop.

Discuss the Sex Awareness Inventory

Sex is distorted in virtually every facet of our society. The open "a-moral" treatment of sex has almost become pornographic. In spite of this, many mothers have passed on to their daughters a semi-Victorian attitude. On the other hand, a host of young Christian men have had no sex education from their fathers and come to marriage with a "notch-on-their-gun-handle" approach. The commingling of these two attitudes in a couple can be disastrous.

It has been my experience that in marriage counseling few sex problems are sex problems. Teach a couple how to deal with the relational problems, and the sex problems disappear. According to Norman Lobsenz in a recent article, most marriage counselors agree. He writes:

> But counselors know that in most cases sex problems are indicative of other conflicts. "When there is trouble in any area of marriage it is likely to show up in bed as well," says John Compere.[8]

However, I am convinced that good premarital sex counseling can help prevent relational problems early in the marriage, which in turn produce sex problems. The SAI is an objective instrument which can act as a springboard for profitable sex counseling.

The simplest way to utilize this test is for the counselor to have before him the couple's corrected answer sheet and the test manual. By coordinating their incorrect answers and circled items (those about which they desire more information), he can be prepared to effectively move through the test with them.

By examining the test with them at this juncture, the counselor prepares the couple for a more beneficial experience when they listen to Dr. Wheat's tape during the next week.

Homework Assignments

Listen to Dr. Wheat's tapes and complete worksheet[9]

These three hours of tapes will accomplish the following:

1. They will provide the couple with an understanding of their own anatomy and proper physiological terminology. This is important. Some individuals cannot discuss sex without embarrassment because they know only street language.
2. They will present the male and female differences and the "how-to" of sexual enjoyment in light of these differences.
3. They will expose the couple to a proper sex discussion and give them opportunity to stop the tape at any time and interact with the discussion between themselves.
4. This will provide the couple with a discussion by a dynamic Christian physician who is frank but discreet.

I am convinced that this method, and at the present time this particular set of tapes, is the best possible means for the average pastor-counselor to conduct good premarital sex counseling.[10]

Have a physical examination

It is wise to suggest that both the man and the woman have a complete physical examination by a competent physician. If either has a physical defect, it is fair for the other to know about it before the marriage. Suggest to the woman that she be sure to have a doctor check the condition of her hymen. It may be necessary to explain that the hymen is a membrane just inside the vagina. If this membrane is too thick, it can cause initial intercourse to be painful. A doctor can determine this condition and with a very slight surgical procedure performed in his office prepare the hymen so that it will yield easily to the penetration of the penis.

Discuss birth control

Each couple should be asked to read about birth control. They should make a list of the various methods and any questions they might like to ask the physician upon their visit.

Fill out family and social background questionnaire

During the next session the counselor can peruse this sheet and raise any questions he notes. He can also think through it more carefully before the last session and add to his agenda issues to be investigated.

Name _____

Fiancée_____

Family and Social Background Questionnaire

1. Comment on the degree of happiness or unhappiness you believe your parents experienced in their marriage.
2. Were quarrels and fights frequent in your home? _____
3. Did your parents solve their problems, cope with them, or let them go unresolved?
4. What was your response to your parent's method of handling their problems?
5. Has your parents' lifestyle caused you to make any determinations regarding your lifestyle in marriage? _____
6. Women: Did your mother ever have a problem with depression? _____
7. Men: Did your father ever have a problem with temper tantrums? _____
8. Do you have mutual friends? _____ Have many of your fiance's friends become your friends? _____
9. Should a man have a night out with his friends? _____
10. Are you sentimental about birthdays, anniversaries, etc.? _____ Would it bother you if your fiance forgot? _____ Was your family sentimental? _____
11. In a social setting, do you mix freely with those of the opposite sex as well as your own sex without being with your fiance all the time? _____
12. Have you discussed where you will live? _____ If so, have you considered:
    a. proximity to parents _____
    b. adequate privacy _____
    c. proximity to school and/or employment, yet separate from each _____
    d. affordability of choice _____
13. Have you discussed the "working wife" and come to an understanding regarding her working, the necessity to divide household chores, her job responsibility, and her associations necessitated by the job? _____
14. Are either of you planning to continue your education? _____ If so, have you thoroughly discussed the problems and decided on guidelines for settling problems as they arise? _____

Name _____

Fiancée_____

Worksheet for Dr. Wheat's Tapes

1. What is your reaction to, and evaluation of, Dr. Wheat's tapes?

2. Did you consider listening to them a learning experience? _____ For what reasons?

3. Did you listen to and discuss the tapes together? _____

4. Sex is good in God's eyes. Dr. Wheat on tape 1, side 1, cited three specific commandments by God as a basis for this conclusion. What are these commandments?

   a.

   b.

   c.

5. List any specific questions you may have or objections to what Dr. Wheat said.

6. Did you find tape 1 as helpful as tape 2? _____

7. Having listened to these tapes as a reference point, please list (each individually) any taboos or incorrect concepts of sex which you have been taught at home or learned elsewhere.

8. List specific questions raised by this experience.

9

Session Five

Discuss Sex

While qualifying the couple for marriage, any previous illicit sexual behavior should have surfaced and been dealt with appropriately. The discussion of the Sex Awareness Inventory provided opportunity for a general consideration of sex knowledge and attitudes. Listening to Dr. Wheat's tapes together will give the couple occasion to ponder their own coming physical relationship in particular and their attitudes toward it.

This session can be opened by asking the couple to articulate their reactions to Dr. Wheat's tapes. The counselor will need to be especially alert to the "halo data" projected in this conversation. The tone of the voice, a glance of the eyes, or rigidity of the muscles may indicate to the observant counselor an underlying attitude which demands attention.

There are two problems that I have found to be frequent among Christian girls which need to be explored. First, they tend to adopt their mother's attitudes toward sex, even though they may not be consciously aware of it and in spite of the fact that in some cases they recognize their parents had a problematic relationship. Therefore, it is wise to ask the girl what she thinks her mother's attitudes are toward sex and how her own attitudes differ. Many women of the last generation still possess a Victorian spirit. This attitude is neither biblical nor characteristic of a healthy relationship. An open discussion of sex will often reveal such an attitude.

Secondly, outside of realizing that men are usually more aggressive, many Christian girls do not have an appreciation of the differences between the sexes. Counselors often hear complaints about the frequency of a husband's desire for sexual relations. While in many cases there are legitimate grounds other than frequency for a wife's grievances, it is also true that a number of women just do not realize their husband's desire for sexual enjoyment is normal.

A concomitant problem with the latter is the lack of understanding by men that the whole of their relationship as a couple has sexual implications. Gentlemanliness and gentleness expressed in a good-bye kiss, a love pat, a "peck" on the back of the neck, a holding of her hand, a simple card or note left on the dresser, an occasional surprise, a simple "Thank you, sweetheart," or "I appreciate the effort you made to make this a pleasant evening for me" will go a long way toward building a responsive sexual relationship. If a husband has offended his wife, a sincere (and the biblical action) "I was wrong in speaking to you as I did tonight; please forgive me" will right a wrong and enhance their physical union. Sex is not a detached source of entertainment that happens to be sanctioned for married couples. It is the unique capstone of an entire relationship. A satisfying sexual relationship grows out of an already satisfying personal relationship. Men tend to lose sight of this important fact.[1]

A thorough explanation of the biblical principles governing sex will foster establishing proper attitudes and avoiding misunderstandings. The first seven of the following principles were compiled by Jay Adams. I have added the eighth.

1. Sexual relations within marriage are holy and good. God encourages relations and warns against their cessation.
2. Pleasure in sexual relations is not sinful but assumed (the bodies of both parties belong to each other).
3. Sexual pleasure is to be regulated by the principle that one's sexuality is not to be self-oriented but other-oriented ("rights" over one's body are given in marriage to the other party). . . . The idea here, as elsewhere, is that "it is more blessed to give than to receive."
4. Sexual relations are to be regular. . . . No exact number of times per week is advised, but the principle is that both parties are to provide such adequate sexual satisfaction that both "burning" (sexual desire) and temptation to find satisfaction elsewhere are avoided.

5. The principle of satisfaction means that each party is to provide sexual enjoyment (which is "due" him or her in marriage) as frequently as the other party requires. But, of course, other biblical principles (moderation, seeking to please another rather than oneself, etc.) also come into play. Consideration of one's mate is to regulate one's requests for sexual relations. But this must not be used as an excuse for failing to meet genuine needs. On the other hand, requests for sexual satisfaction may not be governed by an idolatrous lust.

6. In accordance with the principle of "rights," there is to be no sexual bargaining between married persons ("I'll not have relations unless you . . ."). Neither party has the right to make such bargains.

7. Sexual relationships are equal and reciprocal. Paul does not give the man superior rights to the woman. It is clear, then, that mutual stimulation and mutual initiation of relations are legitimate. Indeed, the doctrine of mutual rights involves also the obligation of mutual responsibility. This means, among other things, mutual active participation in the act of intercourse.[2]

8. The principle governing the sexual play of the husband and wife is simple. Whatever is pleasing, enjoyable, and satisfying to both is acceptable. The *body* of each belongs to the other (1 Cor. 7:4). Neither should demand from the other what is distasteful to him or her, but both should be flexible.[3]

One aspect of my premarital counseling program which has drawn favorable response from nearly every couple with whom I have worked is the suggestions regarding their initial sexual experiences on the honeymoon. In the part of the country where I grew up, an afternoon wedding followed by a long reception lasting till nine or ten o'clock was very common. Such a situation does not provide an ideal set of circumstances for a bride and groom's first sexual experience. Wedding traditions often produce a wedding day fraught with anxiety and an emotional level that drains the couple's strength.

The pastor-counselor should encourage the couple to plan a day that will exclude many of the anxiety builders. The best man and maid of honor should be asked to shoulder much of the responsibility for executing well-developed plans (see responsibilities of wedding party at the end of this chapter). The long and tedious process of opening gifts during the reception should be avoided if at all possible.

One couple wanted to do away with the gift opening, but they knew their families would object. We worked out a compromise of having two of the bride's cousins, dressed like the other girls in the wedding party, receive the gifts as they were brought. The girls would open them and place them on display. As the friends were dismissed following the wedding, the ushers would be instructed to encourage them to circulate among the display tables while the photographer took the wedding pictures. By the time the couple was ready to go to the reception room, the guests who desired to look at the gifts would have opportunity to do so. The girl's parents accepted this compromise suggestion. The couple was very pleased not to have to perform this tiring and time-consuming ritual.

If the family pressures are too great and the couple senses a responsibility to respond to these pressures which result in a long and strenuous day, the counselor should suggest the couple forego the initial sexual experience that first night. They should be encouraged to determine what they think is wise for them and then agree to that course of action.

Remind the man that even though they may have become involved in some heavy petting (and perhaps because of the guilt associated with it), the first time his bride undresses with him and the first time they get in bed together is going to be a difficult experience for her. She may desire to give herself to him with all her heart, but she is going to be somewhat reticent. He should remember to be gentle and take his time.

Some couples have made the mistake of turning their honeymoon into a sight-seeing jaunt. This is poor judgment. Traveling four hours a day and walking from sight to sight another three or four hours is extremely tiring. It also turns the focus on other people and things. A week's honeymoon at a quiet lodge or some resort area where there are things to do together is a good choice. This allows for a relaxed pace. It gives opportunity for spiritual fellowship, social enjoyment, and physical relations at will. In every way possible, this should be planned as a stress-free week or two together.

Another important aspect of the initial sexual relationship which should be commented on is the couple's expectations. They may find their experience disappointing if they do not realize that being a good sex partner is like being a good tennis partner. It takes time, practice, and a learning of the techniques. If the couple views the sexual relationship as a growing one that will continue to mature throughout their married life, their expectations for those initial experiences will not end in frustration.

Encouraging couples not to try all the techniques they might find listed in a sexology book, though these may be perfectly legitimate, during the first year of their marriage will remove a lot of pressure. The practice of these techniques may well come in due time, but those early days should be a time of learning to give pleasure to one another. This can be best accomplished by attempting the various standard positions[4] to discover the one that works best for them and then perfecting it. Communication, telling each other what is pleasing, will speed the development of a mutually satisfying sexual relationship which can be augmented and developed.

Discuss Birth Control

The morality of birth control as a practice was considered with the couple when talking about family planning. At this juncture the counselor is concerned with the knowledge of the various methods and the morality of each. The couple has already been asked to research the topic and discuss any questions with the doctor during the physical examination. However, the counselor should be certain the counselees are aware of the possibilities and understand how each functions. One approach to determining the extent of their knowledge is to ask them to list the various methods and the principle by which each operates.

Contraceptive methods fall into three categories. Category A is those which interrupt the passage of the sperm from the penis to the egg. Category B is those which cause the immediate rejection of the already fertilized egg. Category C is the methods by which the sperm and egg are kept from ever being in the female body at the same time.[5]

Category A:
  1. The condom for the male
  2. The diaphragm for the female
  3. Foams/jellies
Category B:
  1. IUD (intrauterine devices)
  2. Morning after pill (diethylstilbestrol)
Category C:
  1. Birth control pills (oral hormonal contraceptives)
  2. Rhythm method

The pastor-counselor is interested in clarifying the moral implications of each of these methods. It seems to me that the methods in categories A and C are generally acceptable for the Christian. However, it is my opinion that those in category B are abortive and therefore not an option for the Christian. There may also be sufficient evidence of the possible adverse effects of oral contraceptives to call them into question on the principles of 1 Corinthians 6:19–20 and Romans 14:22–23.

Given this information, the couple must be cautioned to choose a method which they can practice in good conscience (Rom. 14:23b).

Discuss Family and Social Concerns

The counselor can take just a few minutes to look over the sheet (Family and Social Background Questionnaire) which they have filled out since the last session. He may well derive no new data from this sheet. Its inclusion in the program is to provide an opportunity to catch any of these particular matters that may have been overlooked.

After talking about whatever is needful as a result of the answers to this questionnaire, the counselor can refer to his file and retrieve the homework assignment in which the couple was asked to list any problems either has had with his respective in-laws. A discussion of the following material with the counselees can set the stage for solving any problems they may have listed.

David Mace has suggested a three-pronged strategy to in-law problems. The pastor can help a couple who already has problems or anticipates them by supervising their integration of Mace's suggestions with other biblical principles and the application of these to their concrete situation. Mace writes:

> A sound strategy must meet three basic requirements. First, it must be fully agreed upon and loyally acted upon by both of you. If one defaults, the strategy collapses and doesn't work. So your planning should be very thorough.

> The second requirement is that the plan should be positive with the objective of achieving reconciliation and harmony, not retaliatory or punitive based on your angry and hurt feelings. The aim is not to reject the in-laws and shut them out of your lives, but if at all possible to win them over and create an atmosphere of mutual confidence and trust.

> The third requirement is that your strategy should take account of the realities of the situation. These you should study carefully

together. No two in-law problems are exactly alike. Yet there are frequently recurring factors that are common to most of them.[6]

Such an approach is biblical. It makes love its aim. And, as Mace correctly concludes, ". . . you can behave lovingly even if you don't feel loving, and the action tends to promote the feeling."[7]

Homework Assignments

Discuss the wedding date

Many couples will already have the date settled. However, there are contingencies that each couple must consider. The counselor should list these matters for them.

1. The open dates that the pastor has relative to the general time they have selected for the wedding.
2. The availability of the church building.
3. The schedule of the immediate family on both sides.
4. The availability of the desired members of the wedding party.
5. The regular menstruation cycle of the woman.
6. Any other particular circumstances peculiar to their situation.

Discuss the ceremony and reception

The couple should be made aware of the flexibility that is possible in the wedding ceremony. That it should be a witness and a testimony to the Lord Jesus Christ is important. The counselor may give them sample ceremonies and encourage them to write their own or to revise the one he usually uses.

The reception can be a family problem. Some non-Christian parents want to insist on a reception that is not honoring to the Lord. Giving the couple the church guidelines (see sample at end of chapter) for receptions and requesting it be filled out and signed when they return next time can help. It may be necessary for the pastor to encourage and direct the couple through some troubled waters with respect to this matter.

Listen to Howard Hendricks' tapes[8]

I would suggest that each counselor listen to these tapes and develop a set of questions for the couple to answer as they listen to them. They should do the listening together if at all possible and fill out the answer sheet together. Hendricks provides a good review of many of the concepts covered in this program. These tapes are suggested for this reason.

Name _____
Fiancée_____

Church Questionnaire Regarding the Reception

1. Will you promise that there will be no alcoholic beverages (beer, wine, liquor) served at the reception? _____
2. Will you promise that any music will be in keeping with the generally accepted standards of the church? _____
3. Will you promise that there will be no invitation to dance given at the reception? _____

Since you have requested to have your reception on the church premises, the official board of the church requires an affirmative answer to the above questions to grant the said request. The board does not desire to limit your personal liberty, but it believes these standards are in the best interest of the testimony of Jesus Christ.

_____
Signature of groom

_____
Signature of bride

Duties of the Wedding Party

Best Man

The best man is the groom's chief servant. He should be ready to give assistance and perform any service necessary to make the wedding a success for the groom. Specifically his duties should include:

1. Attendance at prewedding parties.
2. Attendance at the rehearsal and taking responsibility for any special cues to help the groom through the wedding.
3. Picking up the groom on the wedding day and seeing that the following items are in order and assisting where necessary:

  a. The groom's packing and dressing.
  b. The marriage license and other documents are in the groom's possession.
  c. The wedding ring is in the best man's possession.

4. Attending to the couple's tickets, luggage checks, passports, etc. (These items should usually be placed with the groom's going-away clothes.)
5. Taking charge of the groom's going-away clothes. These should be delivered to the location where the groom will be changing before departing on the honeymoon.
6. Taking charge of the luggage and making arrangements for safekeeping and prompt retrieval, so that there is no delay at time of departure.
7. Taking care of the couple's car and making arrangements for safekeeping until time of departure.
8. In vestry or other appropriate place, delivering "love-gift" to clergyman.
9. Where necessary, signing as a witness to the wedding.
10. Arranging for guests requiring assistance to get to the reception.
11. When requested, acting as the leader/speaker at the reception.
12. Assisting groom to change and being responsible for groom's wedding clothes.
13. Arranging a private farewell with the bride and groom's parents before the usual "escape" from the reception (when requested to do so beforehand).

Maid and matron of honor

The maid and matron of honor are to the bride what the best man is to the groom. Duties may include:

1. Attendance at prewedding parties.
2. Assisting with the addressing of invitation and announcements, listing and opening gifts and, if requested, arranging decorations.
3. Attendance at the rehearsal and taking responsibility for any special cues to help the bride through the wedding.
4. Arranging to be with the bride in time to help her dress for the ceremony.
5. Slitting (or seeing that it is slit) the ring finger of the bride's left glove.

6. Checking with the bridesmaids to see that their dresses are in order and that they have their bouquets before departing for the church.
7. Assisting the bride to pack and seeing that her going-away clothes are delivered to the location where the bride will be changing before departing on the honeymoon.
8. Holding the bride's bouquet during the service, and helping to raise her veil.
9. Being sure that the groom's ring is in the maid of honor's possession.
10. Arranging bride's train before recessional.
11. When necessary, signing as a witness to the wedding.
12. Assisting bride in changing to travel clothes and taking care of her wedding dress.
13. Making arrangements for the best man to take charge of the bride's luggage.

Ushers

The responsibility of the ushers parallels that of ushers in church or other public functions. They are to see that guests are properly escorted and seated. Additional duties include:

1. Attendance at prewedding parties.
2. Attendance at the rehearsal.
3. Arrival at the church an hour before ceremony.
4. Placement of pew ribbons before the ceremony.
5. Escorting and seating of immediate family.
6. Participation in the processional and recessional in accordance with the bride and groom's wishes.
7. Removal of pew ribbons and escorting immediate family and special guests from front pews after ceremony.
8. Escorting bridesmaids to reception and/or driving the wedding party cars.
9. Assisting the best man with his duties as requested.
10. Supervision of guests so as to provide an unhampered "dash for the door" when the couple is ready to depart.
11. Thwarting practical jokes which can be disconcerting to the couple.

Bridesmaids

The bridesmaids should stand ready to assist the bride and the maid or matron of honor as requested. However, specific duties include:

1. Attendance at prewedding parties.
2. Attendance at the rehearsal.
3. Being prompt to carry out all requests and on time for the ceremony.
4. In some instances, they may supervise the display of gifts during the reception.

Though the duties will vary from wedding to wedding and from one subculture to another the foregoing provides a guideline apropos to an evangelical wedding.[9] In most instances, all the members of the wedding party will stand with the couple and their parents in the receiving line which may be formed immediately following the service or immediately preceding the reception if the reception is to be held at a location other than the church.

10

Session Six

Discuss Family Worship

At each session during the homework assigning, the counselor needs to remind the couple of their commitment to the twice-a-week program of family worship. He should check to be sure they are following through. In the early sessions, clarification of his expectations and their responsibilities may be necessary.

This subject will probably consume at least half of this session. Going over their log session by session can be very profitable. The pastor can emphasize strong points and suggest positive correctives for weaknesses. Some things which he is able to discern from this assignment and its discussion are:

1. Extent of male leadership exercised
2. Attitudes toward spiritual matters
   a. Significance of prayer
   b. Relative importance of this exercise to other demands of life
   c. Importance of studying the Word and praying together
   d. Attitude toward pastoral leadership
   e. Relative importance of spiritual matters to each partner
3. Relative dominance of the female

The influence communicated by an in-depth consideration of this assignment is inestimable. Young people hear about the value of family worship, but few have experienced it. This work and its careful scrutiny by a concerned pastor in this highly motivated atmosphere can produce glorious benefits. The story of Ray and Carala illustrates this fact.

Ray and Carala both grew up in Christian homes. Family worship had consisted of table grace and an occasional reading of a chapter from the Bible. During one of the sessions, Ray said, "You know, I've always heard you preach about family worship, and I've read about it, but I guess I just never understood what it was all about. When you gave us this assignment," he continued, "I agreed to doing it because I figured we had to. It sure was hard to get started. We talked about everything—even sex. But I felt awkward suggesting that we sit down and read the Bible together and actually pray together, to say nothing of keeping a record of it.

"I told Carala one night that we were going to begin to do what the pastor asked us to do. I'm going to tell you—it was hard for me to do. I want to thank you, Pastor, for this project. The awkwardness is over and we are headed in the right direction. It is still hard, but we enjoy spending this time with God. And, you know, it has helped our communication in other areas."

A couple should be encouraged to continue this twice-a-week schedule until they are married. By then, it will have become a regular habit. This same regularity can be maintained after marriage with the addition of a daily, but briefer, family worship time.

Discuss Ceremony and Date

The date will usually be a simple matter to settle. Unless they return to this session with some particular difficulty, the pastor will agree to one of the open dates which he had previously given them. Checking to be sure they have cleared the date with the church office for use of the building will prevent unnecessary complications. It is also a good idea to remind them that the rehearsal will be the evening before the wedding day. Set the time of the rehearsal with them.

If the couple does not wish to write a ceremony or parts of it, the counselor should go through his standard service, explaining its significance and inviting their questions and comments. Whenever possible, the pastor can accommodate the couple's desires for changes. No ceremony is sacred in and of itself.

The following ceremony is suggested as one that presents the gospel without the need for a sermon. It has the ring of tradition which most couples desire to retain, but its language is more straightforward, and biblical concepts are particularized.

A suggested ceremony

Dear friends, we have gathered before God to join this man and this woman in the covenant relationship of marriage which was instituted by God and is therefore an honorable relationship. The union established in marriage signifies to us the mystical union between Christ and his church; was given the approbation of Christ by his presence and miracle at Cana of Galilee; was affirmed as honorable by the apostle Paul and therefore is not to be entered into lightly but soberly.

Minister to man: _____, will you take this woman in the marriage covenant, to live with her according to God's ordinance? Will you love her as Christ loved the church, giving yourself for her? Will you be kind and compassionate and forgiving as in Christ God forgave you? And, will you keep yourself for her so long as you both shall live?

Man: I will.

Minister to woman: _____, will you take this man in the marriage covenant, to live with him according to God's ordinance? Will you submit to him as to the Lord? Will you be kind and compassionate and forgiving as in Christ God forgave you? And, will you keep yourself for him so long as you both shall live?

Woman: I will.

Minister: Who then presents and/or gives this woman to the hand of this man?

Father (or other): I do, or Her mother and I do.

Minister: Divine revelation declares that marriage was instituted by God before Adam had sinned. In the wisdom of God, that covenant relationship, given in man's innocency, is adequate to provide for fallen man. It provides for intimate companionship, suppresses permissive affection, establishes a social order, and is a means of transmitting truth and holiness from one generation to another. This is the most holy relationship in life apart from one other, that being the relationship of knowing the Lord Jesus Christ as personal Savior. As in marriage woman enters into relationship with man through committal of herself to him, so we may come into personal relationship with Jesus Christ through the committal of ourselves to him, accepting his atonement for our sins.

Minister: (He shall join the couple's right hands. They shall repeat after him or recite the following vows.)

I, _____, take you, _____, to be my wife in the sight of our Lord Jesus Christ. I promise to be faithful in suffering and in joy, in poverty and in wealth, in sickness and in health. I promise to love you and cherish your companionship till death brings our separation.

I, _____, take you, _____, to be my husband in the sight of our Lord Jesus Christ. I promise to be faithful in suffering and in joy, in poverty and wealth, in sickness and health. I promise to obey and cherish your companionship till death brings our separation.

Minister: (Rejoins their right hands.) The circle, the emblem of eternity, symbolizes the endurance of your covenant. And gold, a substance of beauty and increasing value, is to show the lasting covenant and endearing relationship into which you are entering.

Since this union is to be severed only by death, it becomes you to consider the duties you solemnly assume. If these duties are remembered and faithfully discharged, they will add to the happiness of your life together. Their performance will lighten sorrows and heighten blessings. But their neglect and violation will produce keen misery and heavy guilt.

The duties of the husband will be discovered by searching the Scripture to discover how Christ loved the church. The duties of the wife will be discovered by searching the Scripture to determine how the church is to be submissive to her Lord.

It is the duty of both to delight in the companionship of the other, and to remember that henceforth you shall be one, and to see to it that what God has joined together, no man separates.

Minister: (Prays before each ring is given. The man shall give his ring first. He shall repeat after the minister or recite.)

I give you this ring, _____, as a perpetual reminder of my faithfulness promised before Almighty God this day.

I give you this ring, _____, as a perpetual reminder of my faithfulness promised before Almighty God this day.

Minister: Those whom God has joined together, let no man separate. Forasmuch as _____ and _____ have covenanted together before God and this company, and have pledged their faithfulness one to the other, symbolizing this by the giving and receiving of rings and the joining of their hands, I now pronounce them man and wife in the name of the Father and the Son and the Holy Spirit.

(With hands joined, the couple kneels while the minister prays.)

Minister: Prayer.

Minister: (Invitation.) As _____ and _____ have been joined together, so they invite you to be joined to Jesus Christ as his bride. He has already taken his vow when he said, "It is finished." The Scripture says that God made him who knew no sin to be sin for us that we might become the righteousness of God. You, by an act of your will today, as he enables you to understand your need, may receive him by faith as your Lord and Savior, become the righteousness of God, and be united to him as his bride. You may do this even now by simply confessing your sin and asking him to save you.

Minister: (Benediction.) The Lord bless you and keep you; the Lord make his face to shine upon you and be gracious unto you; the Lord lift up his countenance upon you and give you peace, through Jesus Christ our Lord.

Minister: (Introduces couple to congregation.) I now give you Mr. and Mrs. _____.

For the couple who desires to write their own ceremony, the counselor may advise them that the following items should be included:

1. The purpose of the gathering
2. The meaning of marriage
3. The charge to the couple
4. Questions to bride and groom
5. The affirming of commitments
6. The pronouncement of the marriage
7. A prayer of petition and dedication asking God's blessing on the newly established home.[1]

Solos and/or congregational singing may be interspersed in the ceremony at any natural break.[2]

Laws governing marriage vary from state to state. The counselor should be familiar with those of his state and be sure that the couple understands their legal responsibilities.

Discuss Reception

It is important for the pastor to explain church policy regarding receptions. The ensuing items need clarification.[3]

1. Financial responsibility for custodial services. These may
    be graduated, depending on the amount of service
    requested or demanded by the activity.
2. Financial responsibility for use of the social hall, if any.
    Sometimes this will vary for members and nonmembers.
3. Financial responsibility for personnel working in elec-
    tronics room. This may include price of a cassette tape of
    ceremony.
4. Responsibility to provide all personnel for serving and
    maintenance of facilities and equipment (dishes, silver-
    ware, etc.).
5. Responsibility for all necessary paper products, bever-
    ages, and food.
6. Responsibility regarding the serving of alcoholic bever-
    ages. (This problem should be solved by the promise
    pledge which the couple will return signed at this session.)

The reception, like the wedding, is theirs. But a reasonable balance should be sought between their wishes, cultural expectations,
and practical considerations. Each situation is unique and will call
on the counselor's creativity to guide the couple effectively.

Homework Assignments

The counselor will need to have gone back through his notes
from each session before this hour to check his agenda columns
for any pending questions which have not been covered. Any
items still outstanding can be translated into homework for the
final session.

He should also probe problem areas which the couple have
been tackling via homework projects. New patterns do not
develop automatically (2 Chron. 27:6; 1 Tim. 4:7). Being sure the
counselees are continuing to apply themselves to the methods
designed to produce change and godliness is a vital aspect of
the counseling process. Couples may need to be reminded that
their chief goal is to reflect God and his glory in every aspect of
their lives. Their happiness and harmony will naturally follow.

For the last session, the couple should be asked to review the
various topics developed during the counseling and make a list
of any questions they may still have. To that list may be added
any matters of concern which have not been touched in the
counseling thus far. This assignment will probably be more fruit-
ful if two conferences are held several days apart.

Wedding Music

Hymns Suitable for Congregational Singing

A Mighty Fortress
All Glory, Laud, and Honor
All Hail the Power
Children of the Heavenly Father
Doxology (Praise God, From Whom All Blessings Flow)
Fairest Lord Jesus
For the Beauty of the Earth
God of Our Fathers
God the Omnipotent
Great Is Thy Faithfulness
Holy, Holy, Holy
How Firm a Foundation
Jesus, Priceless Treasure
Jesus, the Very Thought of Thee
Jesus, Thou Joy of Loving Hearts
Join All the Glorious Names
Like a River Glorious
Love Divine
May Jesus Christ Be Praised
My Jesus, As Thou Wilt
My Jesus, I Love Thee
Now Thank We All Our God
O Could I Speak the Matchless Worth
O For a Thousand Tongues
O God, Our Help in Ages Past
O Happy Home
O Jesus, I Have Promised
O Master, Let Me Walk with Thee
O the Deep, Deep Love of Jesus
Praise, My Soul, the King of Heaven
Praise to the Lord, the Almighty
Rejoice, Ye Pure in Heart
Savior, Like a Shepherd Lead Us
Sing Praise to God
Spirit of God, Descend Upon my Heart
Take My Life and Let It Be
The Church's One Foundation
The King of Love My Shepherd Is
The Lord Bless You (Lutkin)
This Is My Father's World
We Come, O Christ, to Thee

We Give Thee But Thine Own
When Morning Gilds the Skies

Selections for the Soloist

A Wedding Benediction
A Wedding Prayer
Bless This House
Each for the Other
O Lord Most Holy
O Perfect Love
O Promise Me
Song of Ruth (Whither Thou Goest)
Thou Glorious Bridegroom (Wedding Prayer)

Instrumental Music

Air on the G String by J. S.Bach
Jesu, Joy of Man's Desiring by J. S. Bach
Prelude and Fugue in C Major by J. S. Bach
Reverie by Claude Debussy
Serenade by Franz Schubert
Trumpet Tune by Henry Purcell[4]

11

Session Seven

Discuss the Agenda Items

The content of this part of the session obviously depends on the homework devised to stimulate growth. Like a computer programmer, the counselor will have to sort and interpret the data which he has collected and develop a program of homework which in this session can give him a reading of the readiness of the couple for good marriage adjustment.

Discuss the Couple's Lists

Most couples will come to this session with one or two questions which will require only a straightforward, factual answer. Rob, for example, inquired, "Can you recommend a reliable realtor who can discuss the relative value of purchasing a condominium for a first home with some objectivity?"

On occasion, however, a couple will dump something into the counselor's lap that will require additional work and sessions. This should not be surprising. The counselor in this program is cast chiefly in the role of instructor or guide who works on the biblical principle that love believes "all things" unless hard-core evidence forces him to question the integrity of the counselees. His consistent building on biblical principles, coupled with the tone of the sessions—honesty, openness, and sincerity—and the

pressure of the last session, may engender the thinking, "This is
it! This is my last chance to get this thing out!" Consequently,
one of the prospective mates may confess a sin carefully hidden
or announce the fearful decision, "I've discovered I don't want to
go through with this marriage at this time or ever."

The prepared counselor will not be shocked by such an experience. He will maintain control of the session and help both
parties handle the exposure in a biblical manner. A lengthened
session and additional sessions may be required.

Determine Postmarital Session

One of my criteria for agreeing to perform a wedding is a firm
commitment to a postmarital session. If the couple is moving
from the area, I make every effort to have them visit an associate
in the city of their new residence or to establish a date coinciding
with their first visit to the area. It is best to establish a date for
this visit during this session. Usually, I endeavor to set this date
three months hence. In the interim, an elder from the church
(who has been assigned to them as an undershepherd) will visit
them. If he discovers anything that demands immediate attention, he will alert the pastor, who will then call on the couple.

This postmarital session is flexible. The pastor may ask them
to return to his office for a formal session. Or, he may plan to
visit their home or apartment. If he chooses the latter and his
wife is sensitive to counseling needs, he may inform the couple
that his wife will be accompanying him. Frequently, the couple
will invite the pastor and his wife for dinner if the latter plan is
suggested. This is fine and need not hinder his purpose. In fact,
it can enhance it.

The observant pastor can gain hints of good marital adjustment by observing the home, listening carefully to the social
chitchat and comments between the mates. After a reasonable
time of socializing (one-half hour), or after dinner, as the case
may be, he may simply indicate that he wishes to turn the conversation to their marital adjustment. If there were any particular problems which demanded attention during the premarital
counseling (he must review notes of the case before the visit), he
should question each one to be sure that adjustment is pro-
gressing. A good way to insure that he does not miss a problem
is to develop a checklist from his own experience. This can be
begun by simply keeping a card in his pocket with the following
list of major areas of marital adjustment cataloged, and a note
regarding any particular difficulty or negative attitude which
arose in premarital counseling:

1. Communication
2. Family worship
3. In-laws
4. Sex
5. Finances
6. Role relationship

He must be prepared to recommend a few weeks of further counseling if the situation warrants it. However, most couples who have gone through this program successfully will be making good progress in their marital adjustment. And, if they are experiencing difficulty in a particular area, they will most likely come to the pastor-counselor before he goes to them. They will already have hope that by the Word of God he can guide them to a resolution of the problem.

Piecing together the suggestions of several Christian medical doctors, I have devised the following suggested check-up schedule. Their suggestions were based on years of medical experience in private practice.

A tri-monthly session during the first year of marriage.

A check-up session after the third anniversary.

A check-up session six to twelve weeks after the birth of each child.

Such a schedule is certainly ambitious. But here again an elder, responsible for a section of the flock, could plan his care around these significant dates. Only if he could not handle a situation would the pastor have to become involved.

Fellowship of Prayer

At his discretion, the counselor may have opened and/or closed each of the previous sessions in prayer. I recommend that this session be closed by asking both counselees to pray, with the pastor-counselor concluding the prayer time.

Perhaps the pastor can move from behind his desk to a more informal position and join hands with them as each prays. There is a compassion and interest communicated in this action which is too frequently missing in our society. We tend to be cold and detached, or demanding and possessive. An example of warmth and offering of affection by the pastor is appropriate.

PART
THREE

Practical Helps
for Premarital Counselors

12

Selecting Family Traits

Jim and Mary had been married for three years when Jim appeared in my office. He was terribly frustrated because Mary had been explaining to him that the only course of action for her was a divorce. She had declared to him that she no longer had feelings for him and without feelings she could not go on with the marriage.

I asked Jim to tell me what had been happening in their relationship for the past three years. The story he told me revolved around family traits that each had brought into the marriage unawares, which in turn had triggered certain expectations that had gone unmet and had in some instances been directly countered.

For example, Mary's mother's conception of being a good wife was being a servant to her husband. She carried her husband's coffee to his chair, polished his shoes, cleaned up his bathroom sink after him, picked up his dirty clothes from the floor, and performed an array of other servant-like chores as her regular routine of life. Her father, on the other hand, was very attentive to her mother. He listened when she told insignificant stories from her mundane existence, he displayed affection in public, he frequently rubbed her shoulders and back while they watched television together, he took her to church, and treated her like a queen, and, while he laughed with her, he never teased her.

Jim reported several conversations he had recently had with Mary in which she had explained the reasons she no longer had feelings for him. These included: (1) He was not proud of her (which meant that he did not display public affection very often); (2) He made fun of her (which meant that he teased her and laughed at her); (3) He did not appreciate her (which meant he had mocked her efforts to serve him); (4) He did not find her interesting (which meant he did not [patiently] listen to her conversation).

Mary had also informed Jim that while she wanted a divorce she hoped that after they had gone their separate ways for a while they could start over and she could regain her feelings to build a marriage again. But at the present she felt too much "pressure" and wanted to be out of the marriage.

Here is a clear case of a couple who have become entangled in family trait patterns. They were from a rural city of 30,000+. They were junior college educated. They had been raised in nominal evangelical homes and churches. They had no addictive vices and neither did their families of origin. They had attended a Bible-believing church together while courting and were married in that church by the pastor. Except for his atypical hairstyle, this couple would have been chosen by the church family as an ideal couple certain to succeed in their marriage, church life, and community contribution. But they were in trouble, deep trouble!

What happened here? The seasoned counselor could certainly hypothesize several possibilities. Since Jim travels out of town for a week at a time, Mary could have become involved with someone at work. It could be that he is not being truthful and has in fact treated her very poorly. It could be that she has been secretly promiscuous in the past and now her guilt is driving some irrational thoughts about her not deserving him. But, when Mary was invited to join the counseling she confirmed the basic report which Jim had given. "So what happened here?" I must ask again.

This case was a clear example of two people unconsciously dragging acquired family traits into their new family relationship and then developing a matrix of interactions and responses which caused Jim to deplete his account in Mary's love bank.[1] It is impossible for a couple to not experience this process. Elsewhere I have written about expectations and provided a homework assignment calculated to surface these and generate an awareness of the dynamics involved for both the counselor and the couple.

However, over the years of practicing premarital preparation as presented in this book, it became evident to me that a positive constructive methodology for assisting couples to own family traits, explore them, and choose among them was imperative.

The following assignment has evolved. It has also been utilized in my classes in marriage and family counseling where I have asked married students to enlist the cooperation of their mates to go through this process and single students to complete it in respect to their own family and to use the results in prayerful preparation of themselves for marriage.

We begin this assignment with the simple diagram which helps the couple to visualize the process (see Figure 5). The two circles which are parallel represent what I call each individual's mini-subculture. This is actually more than just the family of origin, though it is the most influential aspect of subculture for most people. In giving the assignment to the couple, it is good to explain to them that different facets of their lives have provided cognitive constructs out of which they fashion life. I sometimes will say to the couple something like this:

> Richard, there are several things you should keep in mind as you think about your mini-subculture. You are from a fairly well-to-do family in the Mississippi Delta, you have been a fraternity member at Ole Miss, and you have spent almost all of your life in the South. Judy, you are the third and last child of a career military family. You have moved frequently, seen much of the world; your father was not an officer, which impacted your family socially and economically. Your father was frequently gone for long periods of time and your mother was basically in charge of the family most

Figure 5
Select Family Traits

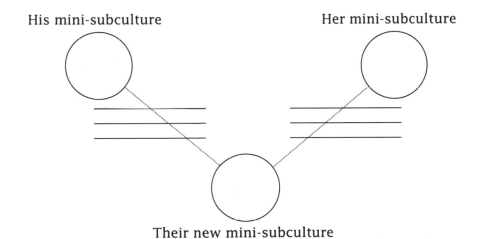

His mini-subculture   Her mini-subculture

Their new mini-subculture

of the time. There are positive and negative traits which each of your environments have provided for you. As you develop this assignment, these contextual facts should be kept in mind. They will help you be more realistic about who you are and what you are bringing with you into this marriage.

There are three steps for the couple in this **Select Family Traits** exercise. Each of these steps should be preceded by a season of prayer. The individual, the couple, should seek God's insight, wisdom, and grace. Insight into what his or her family traits are is important. Wisdom to understand how these have influenced his or her frame of reference about marriage is imperative. And grace to go through this exercise in a manner which develops forgiveness rather than bitterness toward parents and others as well as thankfulness for the good traits provided by parents—even those whose lives issued much hurt—will provide impetus for growth.

Step one is accomplished by each one utilizing a diagram sheet and following these directions (Figure 5). The left circle represents the individual's mini-subculture and the list con-

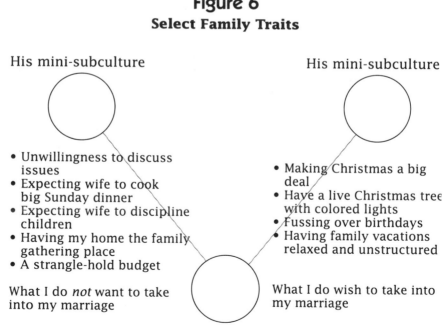

Figure 6
Select Family Traits

His mini-subculture

His mini-subculture

- Unwillingness to discuss issues
- Expecting wife to cook big Sunday dinner
- Expecting wife to discipline children
- Having my home the family gathering place
- A strangle-hold budget

What I do *not* want to take into my marriage

- Making Christmas a big deal
- Have a live Christmas tree with colored lights
- Fussing over birthdays
- Having family vacations relaxed and unstructured

What I do wish to take into my marriage

Their new mini-subculture

nected to this circle represents those traits which this person does not wish to take into his or her marriage. The right circle also represents this same individual's mini-subculture and the list connected to it represents those traits which he or she desires to take into his or her marriage.

Step two requires that the couple sit down together and share the results of Figures 6 and 7. However, this is more than just a "show and tell" process. Each item should be enhanced with cognitive, behavioral, and emotional information. For example, suppose Judy has on her negative list: "My mom handles all the money." When she shares this with Richard she should say something like the following:

Cognitive: I know that this was necessary in our family because my dad was gone for long periods of time and he was out of touch with the real needs of our everyday life.

Behavioral: Mom always became depressed around the end of the month. She knew Dad's check was not going to be enough to cover the bills and she would have to choose whom not to pay that month and put up with the harassment.

Figure 7
Select Family Traits

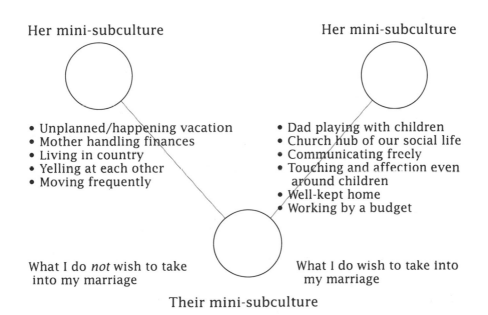

Her mini-subculture

Her mini-subculture

- Unplanned/happening vacation
- Mother handling finances
- Living in country
- Yelling at each other
- Moving frequently

- Dad playing with children
- Church hub of our social life
- Communicating freely
- Touching and affection even around children
- Well-kept home
- Working by a budget

What I do *not* wish to take into my marriage

What I do wish to take into my marriage

Their mini-subculture

Figure 8
Select Family Traits

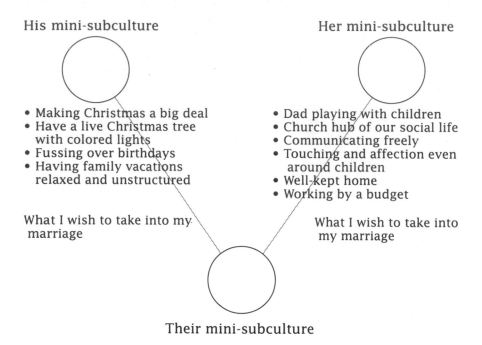

His mini-subculture

- Making Christmas a big deal
- Have a live Christmas tree
  with colored lights
- Fussing over birthdays
- Having family vacations
  relaxed and unstructured

What I wish to take into my
marriage

Her mini-subculture

- Dad playing with children
- Church hub of our social life
- Communicating freely
- Touching and affection even
  around children
- Well-kept home
- Working by a budget

What I wish to take into
my marriage

Their mini-subculture

Emotional: Mom would cry or get angry whenever I would ask for something. She might yell or apologetically say, "You know I can't afford that. I have to pay your brother's tuition so he can get an education." I would be hurt, or angry, or ashamed.

Understanding step two helps the couple while doing step one. It is therefore important to explain the whole process before they do the exercise. As they compile the items on each list, they should think about and jot down the cognitive, behavioral, and emotional material they will need to complete step two. This is a time-consuming task if done comprehensively. But it is also very profitable. Some couples will need your help. I recommend that you have them spend ten minutes working on step one and then go over it with them. This will ensure that they understand both the concept and the mechanics of completing the task.

Step three requires another diagram sheet. This time the couple is going to look over the individual lists that each has prepared and, considering the discussion they have had in step two, they are going to create a matrix of those family traits which they desire to bring into their new mini-subculture (see Figure 8). This process is not simply a matter of compiling a list of the positive traits that each has amassed from his or her family. Such a Pollyanna approach is not realistic. There are some good traits in the negative lists. They may need refinement. They may have been negative only because there was poor communication concerning them. For example, Judy's mother's bill paying may have been necessary and good. But her father's abdication of the responsibility to be an involved family leader, i.e., management of the money and decisions that are contingent on money management may well have left her mother with an unbearable burden.

Step three then calls for a careful consideration of positive and negative traits from both environments. Again, this is a time-consuming process. Successful application of this assignment will demand from you the counselor several things.

Owning: As a counselor you will have to own this assignment. I suggest that you and your wife work through the process together and decide in retrospect if such an exercise would have been (or ends up still being) helpful in your marriage.

Explaining: You will have to thoroughly comprehend the process and be able to explain it to the couple. Developing a good illustration out of your own experience to illustrate each step will enhance their understanding of the process and strengthen their resolve to work through the process.

Structuring: Exactly how much structure is needed varies with couples. You will need to use your counseling skills to determine the amount of structure a particular couple will require. Structure may include the following: (1) directed exercise in a session as suggested above; (2) setting a goal of five items on each side of their individual lists for the next session; (3) going through step two with them at the next session and determining how to proceed depending on their response; (4) gaining a commitment to spend a specified amount of time working on this assignment during the next week; (5) helping them create a structure to communicate about these matters—some couples may become very emotional providing you the opportunity to teach them how to communicate about extremely charged concerns.

Encouraging: Some couples may become overwhelmed with this task. They may be encouraged by several uses of the Scriptures. Sell writes about the negative influence of one's mini-subculture and the possibility of the next generation breaking free from such family traits. He says:

But Scripture also speaks of God "punishing the children for the sin of the fathers to the third and fourth generation of those who hate me" (Exod. 20:5, 34:7; Num. 14:18; Deut. 5:9). While this may appear terribly unjust—that God would punish innocent children for their parents' sin—it doesn't actually mean that. It means that wicked parents will sometimes produce wicked children who will then be punished for their own evil. Scripture distinguishes between the home's influence and the individual's accountability for actions resulting from that influence. Scripture makes it clear that God punishes people only for their own sin. "Fathers shall not be put to death for their children, nor children put to death for their fathers; each is to die for his own sin" (Deut. 24:16).

Belief in the parents' influence—positive or negative—was so strong that the prophets had to caution people from thinking they were unable to break free of it. "In those days people will no longer say, 'The fathers have eaten sour grapes, and the children's teeth are set on edge.' Instead, everyone will die for his own sin; whoever eats sour grapes, his own teeth will be set on edge" (Jer. 31:29–30).

Ezekiel emphasizes that a violent son could come from a good family, or a righteous one from a corrupt home (Ezek.18:1–25). "The son will not share the guilt of the father, or will the father share the guilt of the son" (v. 20).

That is the good news: We don't have to be enslaved to our past. The damage may be extensive, but it is not irreparable. When the young man who could not feel loved asked me, "Will I always be this way?" I could say with conviction, "No, the hope of the gospel is that God can change us; it may take time, but it can happen."[2]

Another passage that can be used is Romans 12:19–21, which teaches us to overcome evil with good. This takes prayerful planning. Prayerful planning takes energy. Executing the plan takes goal setting and personal management. These are godly exercises which when applied to our mini-subcultures enable us to overcome evil with good.

Certainly you as a counselor will think of many other passages which can be used to encourage particular couples by individualized application.

Commitment: Such a time-consuming task is not a normal assignment for the busy pastor in premarital preparation. It takes a solid commitment to the concept spoken of earlier in this book. You must have a commitment to establishing Christian homes, not just performing weddings. This commitment will be tried by some couples who come from less than adequately functioning Christian homes. This particular assignment may stretch your commitment to the limit; also, it may be your best opportunity to help this couple to establish a growing Christian marriage.

The counselor will also have to be committed to engaging the couple in counseling beyond the premarital period if the dynamics of this assignment warrant doing so. For example, if bitterness toward parent or another person surfaces, it may be necessary to either schedule a separate appointment to consider this problem or secure the couple's cooperation to purposely digress to this matter. Indicate how it will have negative effects on their relationship if left unresolved.

This whole process has as its purpose generating a self-conscious marriage adjustment in which the couple chooses what they desire to bring into the creation of their new mini-subculture. It is a prayerful process. It is a deliberate process. It is a planned process. Obviously, there will still be unconscious carryovers. However, a couple sensitized by such a project will be much more likely to recognize what is happening and either, as an individual embark on a corrective course, or communicate with the mate about what he or she is observing or feeling so that a positive biblical solution can be sought.

Placing the assignment at the end of session five has several advantages. First, you will have built an involvement with them so that the couple will be more willing to be vulnerable. Second, they will have already worked through some conflict data and therefore be motivated to "presolve" potential problems. Third, session six usually has some extra time. Earlier in this book it was recommended that each counselor adapt these various components to a structure which is satisfying to him. The principle applies to this exercise as well.

13

Many Weddings, Much Work

There are several developments which may induce you to consider a class/group approach to premarital preparation. The demographics of a given population may begin to produce a large number of marriages yearly. For example, a young rapidly growing church planted in an urban setting may give rise to a disproportionate singles ministry with a parallel rise in weddings. Or, a period of church growth in the past has produced a large segment of the congregation with marriageable children.

The architecture of a building program may result in a community profile which attracts the attention of brides desiring to be married in a "beautiful church." Perhaps your reputation for preparing young people for marriage has spread throughout the community so that parents and other pastors are recommending your services.

For whatever reason this ministry expands, it may well achieve a level beyond your capacity to provide a quality service on a couple by couple basis. When this happens, the answer to this good dilemma is not to limit the number whom you will serve. While in my opinion the ideal is one counselor with one couple for the minimum of seven sessions, a combination of a class/group situation and one-on-one sessions is a workable solution. In fact, I have discovered that there are certain advantages in a group setting.

If the group approach is not a satisfactory means of extending your ministry of premarital preparation, then a viable alternative should be considered. That alternative, of course, is the training of an elder or other responsible leader or a leadership couple for this important task of preparing young couples for marriage. But even if you choose this alternative, several class/group sessions which you co-lead with this lay leadership can tap into beneficial group dynamics.

Biblical Basis for Class/Group Dynamics

Group process in the form of therapy groups has been tainted. Adams[1] rightly critiques this movement and suggests that biblical counselors should not be participants in such activities. However, group process is found in the Scriptures as are principles to structure the way a group is conducted so that it maintains a biblical integrity while capitalizing on God-given relational dynamics.

Since this is not a book on group process, a biblical theology will not be attempted. Suffice it to cite the New Testament church. But even before this endeavor is undertaken, it should be clearly understood that what is being proposed here is not just a class on premarital preparation. That is not to say that teaching, even formal classroom type teaching, will not occur. It is to say that much more than *formal teaching* will occur. It is not to say that the leader is only the teacher, in the traditional sense of information dispenser. It is to say that the leader is the facilitator of learning. The leader(s) will facilitate learning through formal teaching, through experimental learning, through peer interaction, and other dynamics of group process. This is a class that capitalizes on socially dynamic human nature.

First, consider the Lord Jesus Christ. He chose a small group, the twelve. During his earthly ministry the Lord focused on training this small group of twelve men to prepare them for further ministry. Unfortunately so much emphasis has been placed on Christ as the Master Teacher, that the fact is frequently overlooked that his major teaching ministry to the twelve was conducted in a small group context where the teaching process was frequently group dynamic dependent. Lest this chapter become burdensome in length, allow one example of Christ as facilitator to be sufficient. (Perhaps this thought, Christ, one who taught with authority, as a facilitator of learning and not just the declarer, is in itself instructive for us.)

In Matthew chapter nineteen[2] Jesus is teaching in a crowd context in response to the question of the *rich young ruler.* This occasioned his further teaching about the contrast of leadership between the world and his kingdom. As this episode closed, Jesus and the twelve left for Jerusalem. The mother of the sons of Zebedee tagged along and approached Jesus with her request regarding her sons' leadership role in his kingdom. Jesus responds by clarifying the demands of leadership in his kingdom. The group dynamic in this situation is resident in the ten's becoming indignant. That means, I believe, that feelings ran freely—anger, surprise, discussion of the merits of these brothers, etc. Jesus capitalized on these dynamics. He did not criticize the mother of the brothers. He did not criticize the other ten for being indignant. He simply refocused their attention and utilized the occasion as an opportunity to give further lucidity to his previous teaching.

The early church implemented a ministry strategy which utilized a large group assembly for worship, preaching and teaching, and small groups meeting in homes for Bible study, fellowship, prayer and evangelism (Acts 2:42–47). While we do not have a transcript of one of these group meetings, a little sanctified imagination paints a picture not unlike what we experience in such groups today. Human beings have not changed. They too were sinners saved by grace. A skilled leader then used the dynamics profitably, and a skilled leader today will do the same.

A historical observation about this biblical basis may be instructive. Snyder observes that small groups seem to be the common element of all significant movements of the Holy Spirit in church history.[3] The church today desperately needs the sanctifying influence of the Holy Spirit in the area of the functioning of the Christian home. A group approach here may well contribute to this happening.

Biblical Principles to Guide Class/Group Dynamics

Again, an entire chapter could be dedicated to this subject. I will, however, present only suggestions to enable the reader to think through this matter for himself.

Love

The chief Christian trait is love (1 Cor. 13:13). In any group situation, the practice of love is paramount. Emotions surface, misunderstandings occur, communication is not always clear, and each person brings all that he is to the group. This mixture can be volatile. Choosing to love the other members of the group means learning to think and act in their best interest.

Honor

When premarital preparation is the concern of the group, parents, in-laws and other emotionally laden relationships must enter the arena. Discussions of painful experiences with these significant others, particularly parents, must be conducted in an atmosphere of honor. This does not suggest that abuse and other forms of hurt are to be ignored or their consequences unattended. Some of the most productive group work may come from one member of the group sharing how he or she has learned to process a similar hurt, generate healing of fractured relationships or adjust his or her thinking so as not to drag the hurt into the current relationship.

Respect

The facilitator and the group will need to learn how to deal with one another with respect. Respect means that we accept one another at the level of current development. Jesus exemplified this trait again and again in his group of twelve. Even when Peter denied him, Jesus respected him. He demonstrated this by seeking him out to restore him. Within the dynamic of the group, this principle can be very helpful for these future marriages. When couples step over the threshold, all married people know they will discover aspects of that mate which were unanticipated. Learning to respect others in the group who have undesirable traits or seeing one of them model such respect, may well help another to implement it later.

Responsibility

In group process each person must learn to take responsibility for his actions, beliefs, and responses. If a couple comes to the group having had a fight while completing an assignment, the leader should encourage the couple to share with the group how this problem arose. In the process, the group can help the individual take responsibility for his or her contribution to the problem. The group will see more clearly who is responsible for what attitudes and/or behaviors, and the group dynamic can press for ownership and change in a noncondemning manner.

Also, again, in the case of abuse or alcoholism the members can be helped to move from blaming their environment to taking responsibility for their current beliefs, actions, and emotions and planning strategies to change.

Comfort

Paul tells us to comfort one another with the comfort where-with we have been comforted (2 Cor. 1:1–6). A necessary ingredient of Christian group process is comfort. In today's society no group premarital preparation will happen in which there are not some who have grown up in divorced homes. There will often be a couple who is struggling with how to handle their divorced parents—or even a stepparent who is hardly older than themselves—in the actual ceremony. The comfort that these couples can offer one another can provide a context for healing relationships and structuring difficult situations.

Encouragement

Some couples will find it difficult to develop a budget. Some will be uneasy about contacting an insurance representative to get real costs. Others may find it difficult to schedule an appointment to talk with the doctor about birth control. Some may be in the group only because joining it is a requirement for getting married in the church; they may think the whole process is childish or unnecessary. These matters can be surfaced by a skillful leader who uses group dynamics to generate encouragement and thereby growth of the individuals.

Basic Principles of Group Process

Remember, this is a class/group premarital preparation, not simply a class. Information will be taught. But more than this should occur. These couples should be in the process of growing as individuals and couples in multidimensional ways. They should be learning and using information, but they should also be using this information in experimental learning which engages their cognitive, behavioral, and emotional selves. They should be learning from the growth and development of each other in the group. The leader should be modeling many of the dimensions of marital adjustment from his own life—not major story telling, but simple insights accompanied by his own feelings, cognitive development, and behavioral changes.

But for this kind of group process to happen, some important principles should be learned and understood. (Excellent resources to help the counselor prepare for this task are provided by Nicholas, Coreys, and Dibbert and Wichern.)[4] Consider the following basic principles.

Four stages of group development:[5] There are four stages which groups pass through. The **disorganization** stage occurs as the group comes together. Even if the people in the group are acquainted, this stage occurs. They are meeting together for a specific purpose which impacts them with uncertainty. It is helpful to employ some simple approach activities in the first twenty minutes of the initial meeting. A thirty-minute social time with a get-acquainted game could be a useful tool employed before the first session commences. This game could be a customized form of a common party icebreaker which focuses attention on the nature of the group. For example, you may use a sheet with twenty statements. Ask the various members of the group to get the signature of someone who matches the description (see Illustration 1).

The second stage is the **organization** stage. During this stage the individuals are questioning the level of trust they can invest in the group. They are also questioning whether or not this is the leader's group or their group. There are questions as to the pragmatic value of the group. You should not expect that every couple will complete this process. One couple once told the author, "This group is too high a price to pay for getting married in your building." The counselor should be ready to offer individual preparation to such couples (who may be willing to join the group after an individual session or two).

This second stage should be accomplished by the end of the first or second meeting of the group. Since in most cases you will have only six to nine group meetings, it is expeditious to gel the class/group as early as possible.

The third stage is the **organism** stage. Some writers refer to this as the action stage. I prefer to call it the organism stage. This is the phase of the group process in which **the real preparation** takes place. The individuals engage in preparing for the meeting by completing assignments together and come anticipating a give-and-take process in which they will learn and grow and give to others from themselves that which facilitates their learning and growing. If the group is functioning, this will be an exciting period in the life of the group. There will often be long lasting friendships forged in these six to eight weeks.

The final stage is obviously called the **deorganization** stage. It is both an evaluation and a determination stage. Such questions as, "What did I learn?" and "How can I use it?" are raised. Decisions are made about implementing, when and how, in one's life what has been learned.

Group building is essential in early sessions. This has been illustrated above, but needs to be stated here as a principle to be consciously incorporated.

Leaders set the tone for the class/group. It is imperative for the leader to practice the biblical principles articulated above. He must also model vulnerability by sharing both his failures and growth in his own marriage relationship and walk with the Lord.

Leaders must be sensitive to the rate of group development. Couples might drop out of the group if it develops too quickly or too slowly. In rapidly developing groups some individuals may feel intensely vulnerable before they have grown to trust the group. But others, particularly in these premarital groups, may become bored if the group is moving too slowly. The leader needs to be sensitive to individuals and be prepared to do some additional work with an individual or a couple to compensate for the level of group development.

Leaders need to be aware of modulation. Groups are not static. They may modulate back and forth between the stages. A leader needs to be aware when the group sense changes. For example, in a session in which one couple has experienced a great deal of discomfort, the whole group may well have shifted back to the organization stage. Before the session ends, it is important for the leader to massage the hurting (confused and fragmented) couple, preferably through capitalizing on group dynamics, back into the functioning stage. In the process the whole group will be reestablished in the organism stage.

Leaders need to employ prayer as part of the group process. It has been my experience that prayer strategically utilized heightens both group development and the learning process. Some may react to the idea of "prayer strategically utilized." Just what does this mean? It means being sensitive to anxiety, frustration, confusion, hurt or even anger that an individual or the group is having difficulty processing and suggesting that coming to God in prayer may be appropriate. This is a good time for the leader to lead in prayer, or asking one or two others to pray with himself closing the season of prayer.

In such prayer the leader should focus the prayer on the emotional dimensions of the situation and the persons' genuine difficulty dealing with the issue. His voice should project empathy, kindness, concern and confidence in God's active grace. I have found that such use of prayer often facilitates significant growth in individuals and the group. Another benefit of this procedure is that it models this use of prayer for couples' later use in their lives.

Content of Class/Group Sessions

While it might be possible to cover all the various aspects of premarital preparation suggested in this book in six sessions plus individual sessions for the interpretation of the T-JTA or the Trait Factor Inventory, it is not recommended. The T-JTA or the Trait Factor Inventory can be administered after a group meeting, but the interpretation of either should be done in an individual session. If a lay leader or couple is leading the group, the professional pastoral counselor should meet with the couple to interpret these instruments. One session usually is sufficient; however, the counselor should be prepared to invest more sessions if necessary or profitable for the couple. Six sessions would probably be sufficient time to present the suggested material in this book in a classroom format. Nine sessions of one and a half hours will be more adequate to allow for the group process to occur.

The value of the group dynamics develops through the couples sharing their understanding of the interaction between the assignments, group discussions and their experience. One couple may share, for example, a struggle they have had dealing with prospective in-laws. Others in the group may have experienced something similar and offer their solution as an option for this couple to consider. Perhaps the parents of one couple are divorced and they are fearful of the tensions that will occur at the rehearsal or the wedding itself. This surfaces a discussion of honoring parents, while leaving and cleaving as a method is constructed for handling this potential explosive problem. One situation this writer observed with fascination was a couple who admitted that though they had been Christians for several years they had never had a devotional time together. By hearing other couples share not only what they were doing, but also the dynamics of this spiritual time with each other, they decided to do the assignment to have regular devotional times together. At the next meeting they shared their rejoicing with the group as well as their appreciation for the example of other couples.

The material presented in this book and the various assignments can be used to develop the format for preparation groups. (An outline for the sessions appears at the end of this chapter.) Other materials and the leader's experience can be creatively integrated into these sessions. If the pastoral counselor or the lay leader has not had any training in group leadership, it is highly recommended that the books referred to in footnote four be consulted.

The following format for group sessions has been found useful.

30 minutes	Teaching
5–7 minutes	Transition to group structure

| 40 minutes | Group interaction |
| 15 minutes | Summarize and give directions for preparation for next session |

Each couple should also be offered individual sessions if they have concerns inadequately examined to their satisfaction in the group. Remember, the objective is to prepare couples for a Christian marriage. This objective is best met when we are sensitive to each couple and structure our ministry to most effectively prepare them for this wonderful God-given journey through life.

The Premarital Preparation Program

    I. Understanding the Biblical Concept of Marriage (two sessions)
    II. Understanding Your Prospective Mate (two sessions)
    III. Understanding Family Finances and Extended Family Relationships (two sessions)
    IV. Human Sexuality: Relationship Dynamics and Functional Understanding (two sessions)
    V. Understanding the Particular Problems of the Previously Married (when applicable)
    VI. Individual Counseling as a Couple and Explanation of Test Results
    VII. Planning the Ceremony

Illustration 1

Find someone in the group who matches a description. Listen while they answer and observe their expressions. You will know something special about each person whose signature you collect and this will help you profit from this group experience and get to know this person.

    1. My father was in a war and away from home while I grew up. _____
    2. My folks settled differences by arguing loudly. _____
    3. I grew up in a family of five or more children. _____
    4. My family took camping vacations. _____
    5. I lived in a big house in the country. _____
    6. My dad and I spent one time a week doing some fun things. _____

7. I dated my prospective mate in high school. _____
8. We grew up as family friends. _____
9. My parent died when I was a young child. _____
10. I often felt depressed growing up. _____
11. I sometimes get angry easily. _____
12. I have stepparents. _____
13. I shared a room with my sister as a child. _____
14. My father was a super strict disciplinarian. _____
15. My father taught me how to shoot and hunt. _____
16. We played something together as a family almost every week. _____
17. One or both of my parents were alcoholics. _____
18. I would be satisfied to have a relationship like my parents'. _____
19. I had a friend who was abused or sexually molested by a member of his or her family. _____
20. I could talk to my parents about almost anything. _____

14

A Wedding Manual for the Church

Development of the Manual

As indicated earlier in this volume, church policies regarding weddings are often unclear. The pastor has been encouraged to develop policies in conjunction with his official board on coming to a church. Do not underestimate the importance of this action.

In the past two churches where the author has served, he had the responsibility of developing a policy in conjunction with the pastoral staff. The current policy was evaluated. The senior pastor and other ordained staff were interviewed. Data were gathered from long-standing members regarding particular customs of the area and the church in particular. In addition, written materials were solicited from other churches.

This research was freely mixed with the author's previous experience to produce this Church Wedding Manual. This manual may be reproduced and modified to fit most any church situation. Financial figures, people numbers, and deadlines are included simply as examples. They will obviously change from church to church. The manual will need modifications to accommodate the subculture of the area and the church. When such modifications are prepared, the pastor or pastoral staff should submit the entire manual to the official board for approval.

Text of the Manual

> ". . . a man will leave his father and mother and be united to his wife, and they will become one flesh" (Gen. 2:24).

The joining of a man and woman in marriage is the foundation of God's plan for his people and his world. Christians should marry in the Lord and in a Christian church. It is, therefore, fitting that their marriage be solemnized by a minister of the Gospel and that special instruction be given to the couple to prepare them for a life together that is fulfilling to them and pleasing and useful to God.

To assist you in planning your wedding the church has developed and adopted the policies and guidelines in this manual.

1. Applying to be married at the church

At least three months and preferably as much as six months prior to your chosen wedding date an "Application to be Married at the Church" form (see page 181), is to be secured at the church, and the appropriate deposit should be submitted to the *senior pastor.* It is important to make application as early as possible to reserve your chosen date on the church calendar.

2. The church wedding consultant program

After your application has been submitted and accepted, a wedding consultant will be assigned to assist you in planning your wedding. Church wedding consultants are members of the church who have been trained to anticipate all of the details that are part of a marriage ceremony and to be of assistance in all aspects of preparation for the ceremony. They are also familiar with all of the facilities of the church and the policies of the church regarding weddings. Your consultant will be available to work with you in planning your wedding up to and including the wedding ceremony and the reception that follows. The consultant will assist you in making contacts with those within the church who will be involved with your wedding, such as the organist and the custodian. *Please do not call the church office with your questions;* your consultant will be able to handle all your queries. She will also be able to provide assistance and advice in the choice of flowers and decorations. The church wedding consultant is provided for your peace of mind, and she will be happy to assist in any way that she can. If a difficulty arises which you cannot settle with your consultant, please ask her to accompany you to an appointment with the senior pastor.

3. The premarital preparation program

Joining a man and woman together in holy matrimony is a great responsibility. Our ministers act as God's agents on earth within the authority of the church to affect both the legal and spiritual relationship known as marriage. Because they have this responsibility, the man and woman who desire to be married at the church are expected to submit to their oversight.

All couples who desire to be married at the church should be prepared to attend a combination of the Premarital Preparation Program (see Appendix A) and individual counseling with the officiating pastor. The sessions, lasting ninety minutes each, will cover the following subjects:

Understanding the Biblical Concept of Marriage (two sessions)
Understanding Your Prospective Mate (two sessions)
Understanding Family Finances and Extended Family Relationships (two sessions)
Human Sexuality: Relationship Dynamics and Functional Understanding (two sessions)
Understanding the Particular Problems of the Previously Married (when applicable)
Individual Counseling as a Couple and Explanation of Test Results
Planning the Ceremony

Your church wedding consultant will be able to provide you with the dates when the Premarital Preparation Program will next be offered. Call the office (insert number) for the dates and time of the sessions.

The charge for the Premarital Preparation Program (including materials and testing) is $150.00 for a couple who are not members of the church. For members, the costs will be $100.00. Nonmembers should consult their own pastor before attending the seminar.

4. Music for your wedding

Do not overlook the importance of music for your wedding ceremony. Appropriate music helps to make your wedding the worshipful, exciting, special experience that you want it to be.

Consultation with the church organist should take place at least thirty days prior to the wedding day. The organist will be able to provide you with a wide choice of appropriate preludes, processionals, recessionals, and other music for use during the service. You may also wish to have a soloist or an instrumentalist as a part of your wedding. The organist may be able to assist you in finding a trumpeter for the processional, a flutist or violinist to play while the guests are being seated, or another type of musical addition to the service.

The following rules apply to all weddings at the church:

All music must be appropriate for a service of worship and must be approved by the organist and by the pastoral staff.

Because of the complexity of the church organ, the church organist should be used for the ceremony. When another organist is used, he or she must be approved by the church organist.

It is specifically requested that musicians and soloists be present at the wedding rehearsal. As the music is a vital part of the ceremony, it is critical to facilitate proper flow of the entire service.

5. The facilities of the church

The following is a summary of the facilities available at the church:

A. The Sanctuary:	Seats	1000
	Aisle Length	75 feet
	No. of Pew Rows	30

B. The Chapel: Seats   125
         Aisle Length   45 feet
         No. of Pew Rows 13

C. Fellowship Hall: Maximum capacity for sit down dinner is 250. Available are eight-foot tables to seat ten, and six-foot tables to seat eight. Three hundred chairs are available. A caterer must be engaged to supply all linens, china, glass, and silverware; the kitchen must be left clean and ready for the next user.

D. The church has a kneeling bench. All other supplies must be provided.

E. The sanctuary is a sacred place of dignified beauty not requiring "decorations" to make it a place suitable for a wedding.

 1. No furniture is to be moved, except possibly the communion table.
 2. Nails, tacks, wires, screws or fasteners that leave marks, holes, or coloring are not to be used to fasten decorations on any furniture or the building.
 3. Only *dripless* candles are permitted.
 4. All decorations are to be removed from the sanctuary immediately following the wedding ceremony. (If pictures are to be taken after the ceremony the florist and custodian should be so informed.)
 5. When the wedding party dresses at the church, rooms with mirrors are provided. All personal articles must be removed immediately after the wedding ceremony (or the reception if it is held at the church.)

F. Your wedding consultant should be in contact with the florist at least one week prior to the wedding. Arrangements need to be made for decorating the church before the wedding.

G. Rice, birdseed, or confetti may not be thrown inside or outside of the church.

H. Smoking is not permitted in the church building.

I. Alcoholic beverages in any form are not to be served or consumed at any time on church premises.

J. The photographer should contact your consultant at least one week prior to the wedding for instructions. Cameras with flashbulbs are not to be used in the sanctuary or chapel during the wedding ceremony. The wedding ceremony begins when the music starts. It is inappropriate for the photographer to be in evidence during any part of the ceremony. Photographs by time exposure may be made from the balcony. Prewedding pictures may be taken in the parlor, the narthex, or the sanctuary. Following the ceremony, the wedding party may return to the sanctuary or the chapel for photographs.

K. Check with your consultant if you desire an audio or video recording regarding policies and procedures.

L. Your consultant may be able to arrange for your marriage license to be written in calligraphy for a small charge.

M. Any damages to church property should be reported to your consultant immediately.

6. The wedding rehearsal

Even during the rehearsal the wedding party should be reminded that they are in a holy place that is dedicated to the worship of God. The rehearsal usually takes less than one hour. The entire wedding party should attend the rehearsal and be on time. All weddings that include music and a bridal procession require a rehearsal. The groom should give the wedding license to the officiating minister at the rehearsal.

7. The cost of a wedding at the church

Your wedding consultant will go over the specific costs for your particular needs when you meet with her. If either the bride or groom is a member of the church, or if their parents are members, the couple will be considered to be members for the purpose of determining charges.

If you are not a member of the church the following charges will be made for your wedding. All amounts due are to be paid no later than *two weeks prior* to the wedding day.

Premarital Counseling Program (nonmember)	$150.00
Nonrefundable deposit (nonmember)	100.00
(Due with application and applied to facility use)	
Music and Organist	Arranged individually
Custodial Services:	
Wedding and Rehearsal	75.00
Reception (finger food)	45.00
Reception (sit down dinner—less than 100)	75.00
Reception (sit down dinner—100–150)	100.00
Reception (sit down dinner—over 150)	150.00
Sanctuary Use (includes deposit)	350.00
Chapel Use	150.00
Fellowship Hall Use ($50.00 nonrefundable deposit)	200.00
Ministerial Honorarium*	
Use/Breakage Deposit (refundable)	50.00
(Due to consultant at same time as custodial fees)	

*Honorarium: The honorarium is a monetary token given by the bride and groom or the bride's family to the presiding minister in return for the preparation and performance of the wedding service.

In determining the honorarium to give to the minister, it may be helpful to take into consideration that he will invest about five hours in preparing and performing your wedding.

The honorarium is in no way related to the aforementioned fees. If there are any questions regarding an appropriate amount you may ask your consultant for a recommendation.

Any exceptions to the guidelines of this manual must be approved by the senior pastor.

Frequently Asked Questions

Is the Premarital Preparation Program required for all those who are married at the church?   YES.

I am a member of another church. Can my pastor perform the wedding?   YES, but a member of our church staff will oversee the wedding and confer with your pastor.

I am going to be married at another church. Can I still take advantage of the Premarital Preparation Program provided by our church?   YES.

As a member of another church, should I inform my pastor that I am planning to be married at this church?   YES. Our church will normally require that your pastor approve your plans to marry at our church.

When must the fees be paid?   Not later than two weeks before the wedding.

Is it all right to serve alcoholic beverages at a reception at the church?   NO.

For other questions contact your church wedding consultant.

Application to Be Married at the Church

We believe that a wedding ceremony should be conducted, in its entirety, in the spirit of a worship service. The sanctuary is a house of God; therefore, the rehearsal and the ceremony should be dedicated to the worship of God in Christ Jesus. If you concur, please complete the following information:

Full name of bride _____

Address _____
              (Street)   (City)   (Zip)

Telephone: Home _____ Business _____

Church membership _____

Full name of groom _____

Address _____
              (Street)   (City)   (Zip)

Telephone: Home _____ Business _____

Church membership _____

Future address _____

Minister to conduct the ceremony _____

Reception to be held in the church's fellowship hall? Yes _____ No _____

Day and date of rehearsal _____ Time _____

Day and date of wedding _____ Time _____

Wedding approved by _____ Date _____
                (Senior Minister)

_____ Date _____
       (Marriage Committee)

Final approval of a wedding will be at the discretion of the senior minister and the wedding committee upon completion of premarital counseling.

Please submit completed form with appropriate deposit to the senior pastor.

15

A Wedding Consultant Program

Development of the Program

It became apparent to my wife and me over the years that a growing proportion of brides and their families needed extensive assistance with wedding planning. God's provision of buildings with unusual traditional aesthetic value attracted many nonchurch couples to the last two churches we served. This phenomenon generated another need. It became necessary to have someone responsible to facilitate communication between the church and the wedding family.

These two needs gave birth to the development of the wedding consultant program. This program has decreased tension with the wedding family and has engendered a grateful spirit again and again.

The Wedding Consultant Program which follows is presented in a functional format. Each pastor will need to adapt and modify it to his particular setting. He should do this in consultation with appropriate women in the church through whatever organizational structure the women are associated. The pastoral staff should also be consulted.

Text of the Program

There will be a wedding consultant committee chosen by the pastoral staff with the aid of the worship committee and the board of the women in the church. Those *chosen* to participate will be *trained by the pastoral staff.* The wedding consultant will be the liaison between the church and the bride and/or her parents. The consultant, first and foremost, represents the church. It is her duty to see that the wedding arrangements proceed smoothly and in keeping with the worshipful and holy calling of Christian matrimony. She will meet with the bride several times, be in touch with her by phone when necessary, and be present at the rehearsal and wedding ceremony. The consultant committee will meet briefly once a month to receive future assignments and to go over the weddings of the month. There is also an assistant consultant assigned to each wedding who serves as back-up consultant in case of emergency.

Duties of the Wedding Consultant

1. Contact and meet with the bride six weeks to one month prior to the rehearsal. Additional meetings can be arranged as deemed necessary by the bride and consultant. The bride should feel at ease with the consultant.
2. She will meet the bride and her mother at the church and give them a tour of the facilities and discuss possible ways to decorate the church.
3. The consultant should be sure to convey to the bride and her mother that the church and the consultant desire that she have the wedding of her dreams, and the consultant is here to help her achieve that goal.
4. The consultant makes certain that the bride and the organist have met at least *thirty days* before the wedding for the planning of the music. Emphasize necessity for all participating musicians to attend rehearsal.
5. The consultant makes sure the bride understands that there are to be no changes in arrangements seven days prior to the wedding.
6. The consultant sees that all fees have been paid *fourteen* days prior to the wedding. Fees for musicians and honorarium for minister are arranged on individual basis.
7. The consultant will mail a copy of the letter "To Whom It May Concern" regarding policies for the wedding photographer to the photographer. A copy will be sent to the bride.

8. The consultant will mail a copy of the letter concerning the policies regarding decorating the church to the florist. A copy will be sent to the bride.
9. The consultant should inform (in writing) the custodian on duty of the times for rehearsal and the wedding ceremony as well as other information pertaining to use of the facilities at least one week prior to the wedding.
10. The consultant should inform the bride of policies regarding videotaping and if necessary contact video company in question. It is recommended, but not required, that video photographer come to the rehearsal to see how the ceremony is to proceed, and to determine placement of people and best locations for the camera.

Additional Suggestions

Put sign on back door directing wedding guests to use front doors to sanctuary.

Tell guests to use downstairs bathrooms.

Tell ushers to remind people not to take flash pictures during wedding ceremony.

Have bride designate a friend to be responsible (following the wedding) for emptying clothing or appliances from all rooms used by bridal party.

Bride may also want to ask a friend to see about bringing light snacks or refreshments for bridal party such as sodas and cheese and crackers.

Duties of the Wedding Consultant at the Rehearsal

The wedding consultant will assist the minister at the rehearsal in the following manner:

1. She will arrive 10–15 minutes before the rehearsal is scheduled to begin.
2. She will help arrange the wedding party at the front of the church.
3. She will instruct, as necessary, the ushers in the art of ushering.
4. She will meet with the wedding party in the narthex after the wedding party has gone through a practice run.
5. She will help prepare the wedding party for a second practice.

6. She will help rehearse the seating of the parents and grandparents.
7. She will notify the organist to begin the wedding march.
8. She will start each member of the wedding party down the aisle at the proper time.
9. She will make sure the bridesmaids know where the Bride's Room is.
10. She will see that the groom and ushers know where and when to meet.
11. She will work out place and procedure for receiving line after the wedding ceremony.

The consultant must be a woman who can lovingly, graciously, and firmly expedite the control of people. Weddings, unfortunately, are frequently plagued by family tensions. If the consultant is confident in the Lord and projects this confidence she will be able to maintain control at all times. In so doing she renders even those who oppose her a significant service.

Duties of the Wedding Consultant at the Wedding

1. She will arrive at the church one hour before the wedding (or as early as necessary to accommodate the wedding party).
2. She will speak to the photographer to make sure he understands that no flash pictures are to be taken in the sanctuary during any part of the ceremony.
3. She will speak to any audio or video operators to make sure they understand where they are to set up their operations.
4. She will be unobtrusive.
5. She will carry out the plans as practiced and outlined at the rehearsal.
6. She will see that the rooms have been emptied of clothing or appliances belonging to the wedding party.
7. She will see that the florist has removed the decorations after the guests have left the church.

To Whom It May Concern:*
Re: Church Policies for Wedding Photographer

We know that it is of the utmost concern to all parties that the wedding ceremony proceed smoothly and in keeping with the worship service it is intended to be.

The following are policies established by the Worship Committee and Wedding Consultant Committee of the church. Your consideration of and compliance with these policies will be gratefully appreciated and will eliminate the possibility of confusion or misunderstanding at the time of the wedding.

1. Cameras with flashbulbs are *not to be used* in the sanctuary or chapel *during the wedding ceremony.* The wedding ceremony begins when the music starts.
2. The photographer is not to be in evidence during any part of the ceremony.
3. Photographs by time exposure may be made from the balcony.
4. Prewedding pictures may be taken in the parlor, the narthex, sanctuary, or in other appropriate settings. Following the ceremony, the wedding party may return to the sanctuary or the chapel for photographs.
5. In the event pictures of wedding party are required at the beginning of the processional, the photographer may go in no further than five or six rows. The photographer is not to be down front during any part of the ceremony.
6. The committee requests that pictures prior to the service be completed at least thirty minutes before the ceremony begins. This will enable the consultants to use groomsmen and ushers for seating guests, lighting candles, and insure that the wedding party is properly prepared for the wedding.

Your cooperation will be gratefully appreciated. If there are any questions regarding these policies you may contact the wedding consultant, _____, through the church office.

Sincerely,

Wedding Consultant Committee

*This letter should appear on church letterhead. A copy should be given to the bride by the consultant at which time the bride and her mother should be reminded that this letter is being sent directly to her vendor.

To Whom It May Concern:*
Re: Church Policies for Florist

The following are policies established by the Worship Committee and Wedding Consultant Committee of the church. Your consideration of and compliance with these policies will be gratefully appreciated and will eliminate the possibility of confusion or misunderstanding at the time of the wedding.

We know that it is of the utmost concern to all parties that the wedding ceremony proceed smoothly and in keeping with the worship service it is intended to be.

A. Information you may need:
  1. The Sanctuary: Aisle Length is 75 feet.
              No. of Pew Rows is 30.
  2. The Chapel: Aisle Length is 45 feet.
              No. of Pew Rows is 13.

B. Policies
  1. No furniture is to be moved, except possibly the communion table.
  2. Nails, tacks, wires, screws or fasteners that leave marks, holes, or coloring are not to be used to fasten decorations on any furniture or the building.
  3. Only DRIPLESS candles are permitted.
  4. All decorations are to be removed from the sanctuary immediately following the wedding ceremony, except in cases where additional pictures are to be taken after the ceremony.
  5. Please notify the church one week prior to wedding of the time you will be arriving to decorate the church so that the custodian on duty will have the doors unlocked.

Your cooperation will be gratefully appreciated. If there are any questions regarding the aforementioned policies you may contact one of the wedding consultants, _____, through the church office.

                              Sincerely,

                  Wedding Consultant Committee

*This letter should appear on church letterhead. A copy should be given to the bride by the consultant at which time the bride and her mother should be reminded that this letter is being sent directly to her vendor.

Appendix

Premarital Counseling Questionnaire

Name _____
Fiancée _____

General Subjects

1. Name two characteristics which you admire in your mate.

2. Name two characteristics or weaknesses which you least appreciate in your mate.

3. Are you well acquainted with your mate's immediate family? Describe your relationship to them.

4. Give five reasons for wanting to marry your mate.
   a.

   b.

   c.

   d.

   e.

5. How long have you known each other?

6. How long have you been engaged?

7. Does your family approve completely of your choice of a mate?

8. What would you consider grounds for divorce?

9. Is there anything which makes you jealous of your mate?

10. What are your goals or aims in life? Have you discussed these with your mate?

11. How much eduation have you had?

12. What is your opinion of household duties?

13. Give a brief physical history of your family.

Social

1. What are two activities (recreation, social, etc.) which you have in common?

2. Do you dislike any of your mate's family or friends?

3. Should each of you be permitted one night a week for your own interests?

4. Do you think that certain dates (anniversary, birthdays, etc.) should be remembered by your mate?

Family and Home

1. Has divorce occurred in your family?

2. Do you plan to live with your family or your mate's family?

3. What is your thinking regarding the matter of "in-laws"?

4. How many children would you like to have?

5. Who is to be the head of your home?

6. What is your plan for settling family problems?

7. Who is to exercise the discipline of children?

8. Should your mate ever keep anything a secret from you? If so, what?

9. Is the wife in this family going to work?

Religion

1. Are you sure that you are a child of God, having received Christ as your own Savior?

2. Are your parents Christians?

3. Can you honestly say that you believe that your mate is a Christian?

4. Do you believe his/her parents are Christians?

5. When do you plan to begin a family worship time?

6. Do you need some direction in establishing a worship time?

Finances

1. How much money do you think you will need to operate your household?

2. Does your wife or husband plan to work?

3. How much money should your mate have for personal expenses (jewelry, athletics)?

4. How often should a family eat out?

5. What part of your family income should be given to the Lord?

6. Do you plan to buy or rent a dwelling?

7. What is your opinion of buying on credit?

8. Which of you is going to handle the money and payment of bills?

9. How much money should be spent on recreational activities?

10. Have you planned any kind of a budget? ___ Will? ___ An insurance program?

11. If she does work and becomes pregnant, how will the family adjust to the lower income?

Sex

1. What books have you read on the matter of sex in marriage?

2. Do you think your knowledge of sexual and physical relations is excellent, good, fair, or poor? (circle one)

3. Do you think sex is very important in marriage?
   For your mate? _____
   For yourself? _____

4. What is your opinion of premarital sex?

5. Do you think your mate is sexually adjusted and ready for marriage? List three reasons for your answer.
   a.

   b.

   c.

Appendix B

Initial Information Sheet

Name _____

Fiancée _____

Section One

Yes/No (Please answer each question appropriately)

_____ 1. Have you been previously married?

_____ 2. Do your parents approve of your marriage?

_____ 3. Are your parents living together?

_____ 4. Are you a member of any church? If so, which?

_____

_____ 5. Do you attend any church? If so, which?

_____

_____ 6. Do you attend regularly?

_____ 7. Do you pray? Regularly _____ or sometimes _____?

_____ 8. Do you get along well with your parents?

_____ 9. Have you drawn up a budget?

_____ 10. Do you plan to live with either of your parents?

_____ 11. Do you want children?

_____ 12. Do you believe marriage is permanent?

_____ 13. Will you both work?

_____ 14. Does infidelity necessitate divorce?

_____ 15. Do you have any bitterness toward your parents?

_____ 16. Do you know that you are born again?

Section Two

1. Is a marriage performed by a minister different from that performed by a civil officer? If so, why? If not, why not?

2. How long have you known each other? _____

3. How long have you been engaged? _____

4. How much time have you spent in your fiance's home? _____

5. What is your level of education? _____

6. Are you employed? _____ How long at this job? _____ How many jobs have you had? _____

7. Were you ever engaged before? _____ How often? _____

8. How would you classify your home (parents)? Lower class _____ Upper lower class _____ Middle class _____ Upper middle class _____ Upper class _____?

Appendix C

Bible Studies for Couples
Premarital Study of Husband/Wife Roles*

Instructions: Find a time when you can sit down together and study this material. Do all of the work together. Write out your answers and then bring this with you when you come to our next session.

The Wife's Role in Marriage: Read Ephesians 5:21–23

Answer these eight true or false statements:

1. This chapter orders the husband to be in command of his wife.

   (True   False   Doubtful)

2. The New Testament clearly shows men to be rulers over women.

   (True   False   Doubtful)

---

*Here is an example of the type of Bible study which can be developed for the couple's use in family worship. This study was developed by one of my students, Mr. Gordon Schuit, and used by permission.

3. The only reason for wives to be submissive to their husbands is the practical matter of having one instead of two persons to make decisions.
(True   False   Doubtful)

4. The headship of the man in the home is merely a figurehead type, as the royalty of England, and should not be practiced.
(True   False   Doubtful)

5. The headship of a man over his wife would best be described as the relationship of a ruler and his subjects.
(True   False   Doubtful)

6. In the New Testament, the Bible commands the woman to submit, but the husband to love.
(True   False   Doubtful)

7. The headship of the husband is merely over certain areas of life, particularly the spiritual.
(True   False   Doubtful)

8. To submit is the primary command to the wife in Ephesians 5.
(True   False   Doubtful)

Look up the following four passages and decide if they teach the superiority of man over woman. Explain what you think each passage says:

1. 1 Peter 3:7

2. Galatians 3:28

3. Ephesians 5:22–23

4. 1 Corinthians 14:34–35

Look at the following passages and see if you can write out five reasons for the woman being *subject* to man.

1. 1 Corinthians 11:3

2. 1 Timothy 2:14

3. 1 Timothy 2:15

4. Ephesians 5:22–23

5. 1 Peter 3:1

In the New Testament, the relationship between man and woman is viewed from four different vantage points. What would you say the relationship should be, looking at it from:

1. God's viewpoint (Gal. 3:28)

2. The family viewpoint (Eph. 5:22)

3. The government's viewpoint (1 Peter 2:13–17)

4. The church's viewpoint (1 Cor. 14:34–35)

Below are answers to this question: "What should be expected from a man who is the head of his house?" Read these answers carefully and then number them in the order of importance.

_____ He should be mature.
_____ He should be unselfish.
_____ He should be able to command my respect by his atti tudes and actions.
_____ He should consider the effect of his decisions on me.
_____ He should be able to guide me toward a deeper spiritual life.
_____ He should take the responsibility in all major decisions.
_____ He should make the final decisions as far as the children are concerned.
_____ He should consult me before making his decisions.

The Husband's Role in Marriage: Ephesians 5:21–23; Colossians 3:18–25

1. Compare the contexts of Ephesians 5 and Colossians 3. Is there any notable difference between the two contexts?

2. Someone has said that Paul was only reflecting society's view of marriage and that these principles are not binding in every age. Do you agree or disagree? Why?

3. Are the New Testament regulations absolute standards for marriage?

4. Would you say that the roles defined in Ephesians 5 would warrant calling the family a "democratic" institution?

5. What is the major point in this passage (Eph. 5)? Is it the truth about Christ and the Church or the truth about marriage?

6. Someone has said, "There seems to be no doubt that Paul relegated women to a position of inferiority to men." Is he right?

7. List all the points of comparison between man and wife and Christ and the church.
   Christ and the Church   *Man and Wife*

8. Describe exactly what a wife would expect of a husband who is obedient to Scripture.

9. Would you say the emphasis in this passage is on duties or responsibilities?

10. In 1776 Samuel Johnson said, "It is commonly a weak man who marries for love." What did he mean?

Premarital Bible Study
for a Couple's "Family" Devotions*

Yvonne was one of my students at C.C.E.F. This Bible study was created to complete an assignment. I wish to thank her for permission to include it in this manual as another example of how to approach the matter of family devotions in premarital counseling.

Preface

Each assignment will be given in three parts. Part One will be for the woman to do alone during the week. Part Two will be for the man to do alone during the week. Part Three will be for the couple to do together toward the end of the week. At this time they should also share personal discoveries of their times alone.

Each assignment is designed with a specific aim in mind. This will be stated at the beginning of each week's study. The "Together Time" will be taken from the book, *Couples in the Bible,* by Daniel R. Seagren (Baker Book House, Grand Rapids, Mich., 1972). At the end of each chapter are questions and exercises which the couple can do together. There is also a practical "case study" for discussion and a listing of additional Scriptures for each line of thinking.

First Week

Woman alone

> *Aim*—To abandon all dependency on your parents and all criticism of his relatives.
> *Scripture*—Genesis 2:18–25; Ruth 1
> *Exercise*

1. Is the wife also expected to break ties with her family? What kind of ties would need to be broken?

---

*Created and designed by Mrs. Yvonne M. Steenburg, R.N. *Couples in the Bible* is out of print. (A copy may be available in your local church or Christian college library.) This study was retained in the current edition as a fine example of the application of creativity to the development of couples.

2. In what way does a husband replace her father in a young woman's life?

3. On a separate sheet of paper list all the things you do not like about your husband-to-be's relatives. DESTROY THIS LIST!!!

4. List all the positive traits found in his relatives. Save this list and read it every day between now and your wedding day.

Note: Ruth committed herself to Naomi in the same manner we are instructed to commit ourselves to our husbands. To marry a man is to embrace his whole way of life—including his family.

Man Alone

Aim—To learn to treat his wife with strength and gentleness.
Scripture—Ruth 2:4–17; 4
Exercise

1. List ways Boaz exhibited strength in dealing with Ruth.

2. List ways Boaz exhibited gentleness in dealing with Ruth.

Together Time

Read chapter 7, "Ruth and Boaz," in *Couples in the Bible.* (This chapter deals with the extended family and love with high ideals.)

Second Week

Woman Alone

Aim—To learn to give praise and appreciation instead of seeking it.

Scripture—Proverbs 25

Exercise

Pick out the verses from this chapter which directly apply to our "aim." **Paraphrase these and draw a personal application.**

Man Alone

Aim—To learn to give ample praise and reassurance.

Scripture—Proverbs 31:10–31

Exercise

Find within this passage the ways that the husband is instrumental in bringing about these fine characteristics in his wife (see vv. 11, 23, 28).

Note (for both): None of us can live without praise. Praise on your spouse's head will be like water on a dry plant. The praised spouse will flourish and bring you much happiness all your days.

Together Time

Read chapter 1, "Adam and Eve," in *Couples in the Bible*. (This chapter deals with God's order and plan for marriage.)

Third Week

Woman Alone

Aim—To find freedom through submission and to discover and to take your proper place in your new family unit.
Scripture—Genesis 12; 1 Peter 3:1–8
Exercise

1. Show from this passage how Sarah submitted to her husband and correlate how God blessed her.

2. Write a short summary of what "be in subjection to your own husband" means to you.

3. How do you see "being in subjection" applying to your practical day-to-day life after marriage?

4. How will subjection make you free?

Man Alone

Aim—To give her a sense of security by taking a position of leadership in the home.
Scripture—Genesis 12; Ephesians 5
Exercise

1. List several ways by which Christ showed/shows his love for the church and correlate practical ways of loving your wife.

2. How did Abraham shirk or meet his responsibilities as head of his house?

3. Write a short summary of what "the man shall be the head of the wife" means to you.

Together Time

Read chapter 2, "Abraham and Sarah," in *Couples in the Bible*. (This chapter deals with marriage as a lifetime process of building a relationship.)

Fourth Week

Woman Alone

Aim—To outgrow the "princess syndrome."
Scripture—Proverbs 31:10–31
Exercise

1. List the characteristics which make this woman a "virtuous woman." (In everyday language, please!)

2. Which of these characteristics do you share with her?

3. Which of these characteristics do you need to incorporate into your life? Use this list as you plan goals for your life.

Note: In addition to the goals you will be establishing in your marriage it will be good to have personal goals to help you grow and mature as a person.

Man Alone

Aim—To define areas of responsibility and service.
Scripture—1 Kings 12:1–19; 1 Peter 3:1–8
Exercise

1. List ways you can be of service to your wife.

2. Before God, where does a man's responsibility end (wife, family, etc.)?

Together Time

Read chapter 4, "Isaac and Rebekah," in *Couples in the Bible.* (This chapter deals with "love at first sight" and keeping it alive.)

Fifth Week

Woman Alone

Aim—To surrender possessiveness and jealousy.
Scripture—1 Samuel 1
Exercise

1. List the characteristics you see in Hannah's life—both good and bad.

2. What was Hannah's problem?

How did it affect: Hannah?
                       Elkanah?
                       their marriage?
                       Peninnah?

3. List the things God allowed to come into Hannah's life and her reaction to each one.

4. Probably there will not be another wife looming over your relationship with your husband (although there may be!). However, there will be, from time to time, other things or people which will arouse these same feelings—job, church, old girlfriend(s)—even your own children. How will you handle these situations?

Man Alone

Aim—To learn to avoid criticism
Scripture—Song of Solomon 6:4–10; 7:6–9; Matthew 7:1–12
Exercise

How will you handle the situation when you feel your wife is actually wrong and needs a change in behavior and/or attitude? (Take special note of Matthew 7:7.)

Together Time

Read chapter 8, "David and Bathsheba," in *Couples in the Bible*. (This chapter deals with jealousy and does a good job of contrasting the very important "in-the-limelight" husband with the "stay at home" wife.)

Sixth Week

Woman Alone

Aim—To learn to provide a calm, Christ-centered home in which your husband can find refuge.
Scripture—Proverbs 21:9, 19; Luke 10:38–42; 1 Corinthians 7:34; Titus 2:3–5
Exercise

1. Draw a contrast between the type of homemakers Mary and Martha would be.

2. Relate the teachings in Titus 2:3–5 to everyday living.

3. What will you do in your home to make it a "cozy refuge" for your family?

Man Alone

Aim—To learn to view and treat your wife with high respect as a "helpmeet."
Scripture—Genesis 2; Ephesians 5:21
Exercise
   What difference is having a wife going to make for you?

a. Lifestyle?

b. Attitudes?

c. Decision making?

d. Companions?

e. Finances?

f. Job?

g. Et cetera? . . .

Together Time

Read chapter 13, "Priscilla and Aquila," in *Couples in the Bible.* (This chapter deals with the many roles of a woman and handles them in a godly way.)

Appendix

Scriptural Responses for Taylor-Johnson Questions

For the Nervous Questions

3. (1) Recognition of the Lord as refuge.

Meonah Heb. tabernacle, the place for refuge. (Deut. 33:27)

Makseh Heb. a shelter. (Psalm 14:6 cf. Matt. 5:3; Ps. 46; 62:6–8; 91:1–10; 142:1–7).

Manos Heb. a way of escape. (2 Sam. 22:1–51; Ps. 59:16–17; 142:4 [human contrasted with divine 142:5]; Jer. 16:19)

Note Heb. 6:18–20 in this discussion.

(2) Respond accordingly to the difficulty.

If only a momentary upset, claim *manos.* If a frequent occurrence of upset, claim *makseh.* If it is a life-dominating problem, claim *meonah.* Note the promise of Deut. 33:27 with the corresponding responsibility for the believer, and cf. 2 Cor. 13:3–5.

(3) Regard and respond to the person. (Phil. 4:6–8; after this is committed to God in love, Col. 3:12–15)

7. (1) Recognize that the thought life is a strategic battle-
ground for the spiritual warfare. (2 Cor. 10:3–5; Eph.
6:10–18; Isa. 26)

(2) Rest in the Lord. (Matt. 11:28–30)

(3) Commit it to the Lord. (Ps. 37:5; Prov. 16:3)

15.(1) Determine the extent of annoyance and respond
according to God's design of action for different
kinds:

Mazowk Heb. anguish caused by confinement, e.g., 1
Sam. 22:2.

Response: Ps. 25:17; 107:6–31. Lord will give peace if
the believer responds. (Phil. 4:6–8; 1 Peter 5:7–9)

Zar Heb. an annoyance caused by either an enemy, or
the stress if a pebble-in-the-shoe kind of irritation.
(2 Sam. 22:7)

Response: 2 Sam. 22:7; Ps. 18:6; 120.

(2) If the response is a confinement situation, compare
Paul's response: Acts 16:25; 1 Thess. 5:15–18. If the
noise is by one whom you consider an enemy: Matt.
5:43–48.

17.   (Ps. 131; Rom. 5:1–11; Isa. 26:3; Rom. 15:13–14; Phil.
4:6–8)

25.   (Gen. 26:26; Exod. 14:13; 1 Sam. 12:7; Ps. 27; Prov.
29:25; Isa. 41:10–20; Heb. 13:6, 8; Ps. 37; 73; 20)

27.   (James 3:17; Gal. 5:22–26; Prov. 14:29; 21:5; 29:20;
James 1:19–27; Eccles. 5:2; 7:8–9 cf. Rom. 5:1–11;
Prov. 19:1–3, 8)

32.   (John 16:33; Heb. 13:5b–6, 8; Phil. 4:6–8; 1 Peter 5:10)

35.   (Matt. 19:14, cf. Lord's response, Mark 10:15–16)

(1) If the person's own children: Deut. 6:7; Prov. 22:6;
Eph. 6:4; Col. 3:21; 1 Tim. 3:4, 12; Titus 2:4.

(2) If other's children, respond as with number 32 and
incorporate Jesus' response sincerely. (Mark 10:16)

38.   (Gen. 4:6–7; Eph. 4:31–32; Col. 3:8–10; 1 Tim. 2:8;
James 1:19–20, 21) Note the usage of *thumos* in Gal.
5:20; a sudden outburst is characteristic of the flesh
and not walking by means of the Spirit.

40.   Renewing the mind on the truth of God. (Rom. 12:1–3;
Isa. 26:3; Phil. 4:6–8; Eph. 4:22–23; Ps. 3, 4)

44.   (1 John 4:16–18; Matt. 6:33–34; Isa. 8:12; 2 Tim. 1:7;
John 14:27; 16:33)

47.   (Matt. 6:24–34; 1 Peter 5:6–7) If ill, have them turn to
either John 9:1–5; if there is no sin in life, or, if sin in
the life: Ps. 32:3–5; 38:3–18.

57. Eccles. 4:5–6; 7:5–6; Prov. 22:24–26. Warnings. Implement 47 for response to this.
62. A combination of 57, 44, 32.
65. *Damam* Heb. to be silent. (Ps. 37:7; 62:5)
   Hamah Heb. to hold your peace. (Hab. 2:20) Rest in the Lord!
   Nuach Heb. to settle down. (Josh. 1:13, 15; Hab. 3:16)
   Shakan Heb. to reside. (Ps. 16:9)
   Shalom Heb. to be peace. (Ps. 38:3) Wait on the Lord!
   Kul Heb. to writhe in waiting. (Ps. 37:7)
   Yakal Heb. to hope in waiting. (Ps. 69:3; Mic. 7:7)
   Kawah Heb. to wait in expectation. (Ps. 25; 27:14; 37:9, 34; 130:5; Prov. 20:22; Isa. 40:31; Lam. 3:25; Hos. 12:6)
   Shabar Heb. to scrutinize in expectation. (Ps. 123:2)
   Shamar Heb. to observe in waiting. (Ps. 59:9)

   It can be seen from the above that God has designed for the restless a program of service for others in a ministry of intercession and prayer (Phil. 4:6–8). Usually the constant workaholic is self-centered, contending for praise even in actions done for others. It is for this reason that the Lord in Matthew 6:1–18 stresses the principle of "secret" prayer. (1 Thess. 5:16)

68. (Gal. 5:22–26; 1 Cor. 6:12–13; 9:24–27; 10:13)
70. (Ps. 3–4) Make sure sins are being confessed. (Ps. 32; 38; 51)
72. (Gal. 5:22–26; James 3:13–18)
75. 65, 72, 70, 57, 47.
80. 3, 7, 15, 38, 57.

For the Depressive Questions

94. (1) Recognize the Lord never changes in his loving concern for us. (Deut. 31:6–8; Josh. 1:5–9; Heb. 13:5–8; Matt. 6:24–34)
   (2) Realize the potential promise of future service for Christ. Remind the person of the example of Jephthah being an outcast who became a judge in Israel, in Judges 11.
   (3) Allow the Holy Spirit to develop the spiritual gifts that you have in anticipation for this work. (Rom. 12:3–21; 1 Cor. 12–14; Eph. 4:11–16)

(4) If you are performing the first three, then you will be fulfilling Gal. 6:1–4, 9–10; 1 Thess. 5:11–23 and will be showing yourself to be friendly. (Prov. 18:24)

97.(1) May result from a partying spirit with a realization that a leader has fallen from his pedestal. Show 1 Cor. 3 and may want to mention Heb. 11 cf. Heb. 12:1–2 pointing out that each of these men of faith had failures.

(2) May be just a general symptom. Read Ps. 42–43. Point out the power of God to heal the hurt: Ps. 147, 34, background of Ps. 3 cf. 2 Sam. 15, then read Ps. 3. If person really discouraged, explain background to Michtam's Ps. 56 (cf. 1 Sam. 21:10); 57 (cf. 1 Sam. 22:1; 24:3); 58 (cf. 1 Sam. 24:9–22); 59 (cf. 1 Sam. 19). Have person read them.

101.   (1) Needs hope in biblical sense:
Kul Heb. to writhe in hope. (Lam. 3:26)
Yakal Heb. to have hope in waiting. (Ps. 31:24; 33:18, 22; 38:15; 42:5, 11; 43:5; 119:49, 81, 114; 39:7; Prov. 10:28; 13:12)
Kesel Heb. a confident hope. (Ps. 78:7)
Mibtak Heb. an assured, confident, secure, hope. (Jer. 17:7–8)
Makseh Heb. a place of trust, a shelter. (Joel 3:16)
Seber Heb. an expectation, hope. (Ps. 119:116)
Tiqvah Heb. a thing I long for. (Ps. 71:5 cf. Matt. 6:31)
(2) Point out that the source of hope is the Word of God. (Ps. 1; cf. Jer. 17:7–8)
(3) Point out that implementing the Word into life produces hope. (Rom. 5:1–11)
(4) Point out that our hope is wrapped up in Christ. (1 Peter 1:3; 1 Thess. 5:8; Rom. 8:24–39)

104.   (Isa. 8:12; 1 John 4:18; 2 Tim. 1:7; John 14:27) Note answer to 25 under "Nervous."

116.   Josh. 1:8. *sakal* Heb. expertise; used elsewhere: (a) to have insight, Jer. 9:23–24; (b) to give insight, Ps. 32:8; (c) to act wisely, Amos 5:13–14; (d) to have success, Josh. 1:8; Jer. 10:21; (e) to cause success, 1 Kings 2:3.

118.   (Eccles. 3:10–11; 7:14; 3:12, 13, 22; 5:18, 19; 8:15; 9:7–9) The teaching is that life is a precious gift from God to be enjoyed. Not a false epicureanism! The divine response by the believer should be Eccles. 9:10; Eph. 5: 15–17; Phil. 1:21.

127. Revel in the love of God: Rom. 8. If God has done all of this, how can anyone say, "Nobody cares"?
130. (Phil. 3:8–21; 4:4–9) Point out Paul's experience while writing the Book of Philippians.
135. (Ps. 3–4; 34: 18–19; Isa. 41:10–20; 61:1–2; Luke 4:18–21; I Peter 5:7–10)
137. (Rom. 15:13–14) Stress the function of the Holy Spirit as *paraclete,* Greek, one called alongside to help. (John 14:16–18, 26–31; 16: 7–33) Note God's design in giving us problems: 2 Cor. 1:3–12; 12:1–10; 4:7–18.
139. (2 Cor. 1:8–10; 1 Kings 19; Rom. 8:17; James 5:10; 1 Peter 2:20; 3:14; 4:16; 5:10; 1 Cor. 10:12–13)
142. (2 Cor. 1:9–10; Rom. 5:1–5; Ps. 42–43; Rom. 8:5–17; 2 Peter 1:3–12; 2 Cor. 9:8; Phil. 1:6; Philem. 1:6; 1 Thess. 5:24; Heb. 7:25; John 14:12)
146. (Jer. 1; Josh. 1:5–9; 1 Kings 2:1–3; Heb. 13:5–8; Eph. 6:6; Col. 3:22)
152. 146, 135, Ps. 23.
155. 94, 97, 116, 118, 127, 130, 135, 137, 139, 142, 146.
159. Note 118. (Prov. 15:13, 15; 17:22; Deut. 12:7, 12, 18; 14:26; 16:11, 14, 15; 26:11; Ps. 5:11; 31:7; 33; 97:12; Eccles. 11:9; Phil. 4:4; 3:1; 1 Thess. 5:16)
169. (Ps. 139; Eph. 2:10; Jer. 1; Gen. 1:26–28; Isa. 44:24; Eccles. 11:5; Rom. 8:18–39; John 3:8–21)
171. (2 Sam. 11; Prov. 19:24, 21:25; 22:13; 24:30–34; 24:12–16; Rom. 12:11; Heb. 6:12)
176. 130, 127, 135, 142.
180. 94, 97, 101, 116, 118, 127, 130, 135, 137, 142, 147, 152, 159, 169, 171.

For the Active-Social Questions

2. (Gal. 6:10; 1 Thess. 5:15)
6. (1 Tim. 4:8)
9. See 2, 6. (Gal. 6:1–10; James 5:16; Luke 10:29–42 [Keep biblical balance] Mark 6:31)
13. Note 2, 9. (Prov. 17:17; 18:24; 27:6, 9; Matt. 11:19; John 15:14–15)
16. 1 Tim. 4:8; principle of exercise. (1 Cor. 9:24–27; Heb. 12:1–2)
19. (Mark 6:31; Luke 10:29–42)
24. (Matt. 13:2; 14:14; 15:10; 17:14; 20:31; 21:8; 22:23; 23:1, Jesus' example beside Luke 10:29–42 and Mark 6:31; 1 Peter 2:21; 1 John 2:6)
26. 24, 6.

28.   (Heb. 13:2; Rom. 12:13; 1 Peter 4:9)
33.   (Isa. 28:16; Prov. 19:2; 25:8–9)
37.   (Eccles. 7:16; Titus 1:7)
42.   (Gal. 6:1–3; Rom. 14:7, 19–15:4; Phil. 2:20, 21)
45.   (Prov. 6:6; 13:4; 20:4; 12:24, 27; 18:9; 19:23–24; 21:25; 22:12–13; Heb. 6:11)
55.   (Prov. 10:4; 12:24, 27; 13:4; 21:5; 27:23; 2 Cor. 8:22; 1 Cor. 11:1)
64.   Prov. 18:24; note 24.
76.   2, 6, 9, 13, 24, 28, 42, 45.
78.   (James 1:19–27; Prov. 8:6; 23:16; Eph. 4:16; Rom. 15:13–14; Mal. 3:16; Ps. 107:2)
82.   See 76.
87.   See 64.
86.   See 76.

For the Expressive-Responsive Questions

91.   (Eph. 4:32; Rom. 12:10; 1 Peter 5:14)
93.   Explanation of biblical love, 1 Cor. 13.
98.   If this is true in the assembly, how much more within the family? Rom. 16:16; 1 Cor. 16:20; 2 Cor. 13:12; 1 Thess. 5:26; 1 Peter 5:14. Husband and wife, 1 Cor. 7:5; note: Mark 10:19.
100.   (Eph. 4:16, 32; 1 Peter 3:8)
105.   Note response to 91, 93, 100.
110.   Acts 10:15 principle. Gen. 2:24; Matt. 19:6 with the husband-wife relationship, 1 Cor. 7:5.
112.   (Ps. 8) If one is unappreciative of beauty from God is . . . also of her servants? 1 Thess. 5:12–13.
121.   (Prov. 18:24) See "Active-Social."
128.   See "Nervous" 35.
131.   (James 5:16; 2 Tim. 1:7)
138.   (Prov. 17:18)
141.   See "Active-Social" 75.
143.   2 Cor. 1:3–11. Have you been afflicted?
148.   (Col. 3:15)
151.   (1 Thess. 4:11; 2 Thess. 3:12) Women: 1 Cor. 14:28, 34; 1 Tim. 2:11–12; in the church: Phil. 2:4)
157.   (Rom. 12:10)
163.   (James 5:16; Rom. 12:15)
170.   Note 76 in "Active-Social."
174.   98, 100, 148, 112.
178.   91, 93, 98, 100, 110, 121.

For the Sympathetic-Indifferent Questions

1. (Eph. 4:32; Matt. 6:12; 18:27, 32; Luke 17:3; Col. 3:13; Luke 7:40–43)
4. (Job 22:29; Eccles. 7:2; Phil. 2:1–4; James 1:27; 1 Peter 3:8; Luke 10:30–37)
12. (Rev. 1:6; 1 Peter 2:9; Heb. 5:2; 1 Thess. 5:14; 1 Cor. 13; 1 Sam. 12:23; 23:21; Gal. 6:2; Rom. 15:1–4; 1 John 4:7)
18. (Gal. 6:10; 1 Thess. 5:15)
21. (James 1:27; 1 Cor. 13)
36. (Eph. 4:16; Acts 18:27, NASB; 1 Thess. 2:11; 5:14, NASB)
46. (Phil. 2:4; Rom. 15:1–4)
49. (1 Thess. 5:14; Deut. 6:7; 11:19; 31:13; Prov. 22:6; 13:24; 19:18; 22:15; 23:13–14; 29:15–17; Eph. 6:4; Col. 3:21)
51. See 1, 4, 12, 18, 21, 36, 46.(Phil. 4:9 cf. 1 Thess. 2:7–8)
53. (Phil. 2:4; Job 13:5; 16:3; Prov. 10:14; 12:23; 13:3; 14:3; 15:2, 7, 14: 18:13; 29:11; Eccles. 10:14)
57. (Prov. 8:14; Rom. 12:15; 2 Cor. 1:3–11; Rom. 5:1–11)
60. See Scriptures under 1.
69. Balance. Note Gal. 5:22–26; 1 Cor. 13.
71. (Phil. 2:4; 1 Cor. 13; Gal. 6:10; 1 Thess. 5:14–15)
73. See Scriptures under 51.
81. (Gal. 6:10; 1 Thess. 5:14–15; Rom. 13:1–7; 1 Tim. 2:1–2)
84. Principle of Deut. 20:19–20; 25:4; 22:1–10; Exod. 21:28–36; point out that disregard of animals could lead to people: 1 Cor. 9:9; 1 Tim. 5:18.
86. (Phil. 2:4; 2 Cor. 5:15; Rom. 15:1–4; Gal. 6:1–10; 1 Thess. 5:11–24; Rom. 12:10–21)
88. See 51; James 1:27; compare God's attitude: Isa. 46:4; cf. Eph. 5:1.
90. (Matt. 18:15–35; Eph. 4:32; Col. 3:13)

For the Subjective Questions

99. (Ps. 119:66; Phil. 4:8–9; 2 Cor. 13:5; 1 Cor. 9:27; 1 Thess. 5:8; see Rom. 12:2; Eph. 4:23)
102. (Phil. 2:4–12; Ps. 42–43; Eccles. 7:16; Col. 3:1–17)
107. (James 3:13–18; Prov. 2; note wisdom in Prov. 9:10; 10:8–14; 11:12; 13:14–16; Hos. 14:9; Rom. 15:13–14; Eph. 5:15–17; Col. 3:10–18)

109.   (2 Tim. 2:7; Prov. 14:29; 19:2; 21:5; 25:8; 29:20;
       Eccles. 5:2; 7:9)
114.   (2 Cor. 13:5; Phil. 4:8–9)
119.   (Gal. 5:22–26; 1 Cor. 13; John 13:34)
123.   (1 John 3:20–21; Ps. 119:5–6; Isa. 50:7; 1 Peter 4:16)
134.   (Ps. 37:1; Prov. 3:31; 23:17; Rom. 13:13–14; Gal.
       5:22–26; Titus 3:3; James 3:14–16)
136.   (2 Tim. 2:7; Rom. 14:18; Eph. 5:10; 1 Peter 2:20)
140.   (Col. 3:13; Lev. 19:18; Prov. 20:22; 24:29; Rom. 12:17;
       1 Thess. 5:15; 1 Peter 3:9; see also forgiveness, Mark
       11:25; Luke 17:4; Eph. 4:32)
144.   See 99, 107.
150.   (James 3:1–8; Rom. 12:18–21)
154.   (1 Cor. 13)
160.   See 109 and Rom. 13:1–7.
162.   (Gal. 5:22–26; Prov. 16:32; 25:28; James 3:1–18)
165.   (Eccles. 11:4; 2 Cor. 13:5)
167.   See 123.
173.   See 99, 107, 109, 162.
175.   (Col. 2:16; 1 Cor. 4:5; 2 Cor. 13:5)
179.   (Deut. 10:17; 2 Chron. 19:7; Col. 3:25; James 1:17; 1
       Peter 1:17; Matt. 5:48; Eph. 5:1)

For the Dominant Questions

5.   (1 Sam. 3:19; Luke 2:52; Eph. 5:1; Ps. 32:9)
8.   (Eph. 5:21; see Scriptures in Deut. 31:5; Josh. 1:5–8;
      Heb. 13:5–8)
10.   See "Active-Social" 16, 76; "Depressive," Light-hearted
      150; and 5 above.
14.   Favorable trait: Matt. 5:9; Rom. 12:18. Unfavorable: 1
      Tim. 4:12; 1 Thess. 5:18; Eph. 4:30.
23.   Favorable: 1 Cor. 9:24; 10:31. Unfavorable: 1 Cor. 12;
      Eph. 4; Rom. 12:4.
29.   Favorable: 1 Peter 5; 1 Tim. 3; Titus 1. Unfavorable:
      23 and James 3:1.
31.   (Ezek. 34:18; Hos. 10:1; Phil. 2:4–12)
34.   (1 Peter 2:20–23; 4:16–19; Eph. 4:28–32; Phil. 4:11;
      John 6:43; 1 Cor. 10:10; Phil. 2:14)
39.   (Eph. 6:6; Col. 3:22; Rom. 12:11)
41.   (Gal. 5:22–23; James 1:19–21; Eph. 4:2; 1 Tim. 3:3; 2
      Tim. 2:24; Titus 3:2; James 3:17)
43.   See 41.
48.   See "Depressive" 142.
50.   (Rom. 15:13–14)

52. (Gal. 5:22–26; Rom. 8:11–16)
54. See 41.
59. (1 Peter 5:3, PHILLIPS; Titus 1:7; Phil. 2:4)
63. See 52.
67. (Gal. 5:22–26; James 3:13–18) See 59; rather, Rom. 12:7; 1 Tim. 3:2. If so have the gift.
74. (1 Tim. 3:3; 2 Tim. 2:24; Titus 3:2; James 3:17) See "Depressive" 142
85. See 52.

For the Hostility Questions

145. (Titus 1:8; Gal. 5:23–26) Also note the same Scriptures used in 117: A person who is too lenient is not self-controlled.
147. (3 John 9–12) Note Scriptures for 106; also 117.
149. (Gal. 5:23–26; 6:16; Heb. 4:16; Matt. 9:13; 12:7; 23:23; Luke 10:25–37; Col. 3:12–15; Luke 6:35–36; James 2:13; Rom. 12:8; Matt. 6:12; 18:15–21; Luke 17:3; Eph. 4:32)
156. Note first Scriptures for 92, 103, 108, 111, 113, 117, 125, 129, 149. (James 2:4; Matt. 7:1–5)
158. Note the answer to 156. Eph. 4:32. (1 Cor. 13:4; 2 Cor. 6:6; Gal. 5:22–26; Col. 3:12–15)
161. Note answer to 158. Point out scriptural meaning of highmindedness: *tuphoo:* to be wrapped up in smoke, hence, "in one's self." (1 Tim. 3:6; 6:4; 2 Tim. 3:4)
164. (Gal. 5:22–26; 1 Tim. 3:3; James 1:5; 3:17; 1 Peter 2:18; James 1:19; 3:1–18; Phil. 4:5) Note Heb. 5:2. Principle of divine forgiveness, Matt. 18:20–21; Luke 6:35–36. Note the Scripture on 92, 103, 117, 129, 149.
92. "And be kind to one another, tender-hearted, forgiving each other, just as God in Christ also has forgiven you." Eph. 4:32. "To sum up, let all be harmonious, sympathetic, brotherly, kind-hearted and humble in spirit; not returning evil for evil, or insult for insult, but giving a blessing instead; for you were called for the very purpose that you might inherit a blessing." 1 Peter 3:8–9, NASB.
96. More than likely this is only the symptom, with the root cause being hypocrisy.

Put Off Scriptures:
Matt. 23:28; Mark 12:15;
Luke 12:1ff.;
I Tim. 4:2ff

Put On Scriptures:
James 5:17–18;
1 Peter 2:2–10cf.
Matt. 6:1–18; 5:43–48.

103. *Put Off Scriptures:*
Eph. 4:17–20;
Prov. 15:18

Put On Scriptures:
Eph. 4:16, 24–27;
Prov. 16:32; 15:1; 14:29;
29:11

106. The Scriptures for anger apply here as above. Also note James 1:19; Rom. 12:19; Titus 1:7; 1 Pet. 5:3 cf. 1 Thess. 5:12–15 (put off and put on is here).

108. (Eph. 4:16–32; Rom. 14:13–19; 15:2–6) 1 Cor. 14:26—principle. Remember 1 Cor. 8:1 and 1 Peter 3:10–12; 4:8.

111. (Gal. 5:23–26; 2 Peter 1:3–11; Titus 1:8; 1 Cor. 9:25)

113. (Gal. 5:23–26; Titus 3:2; Col. 3:12–15; 1 Tim. 6:11; Gal. 6:1; 2 Tim. 2:25; Ps. 37:11)

117. (Gal. 5:22–26; Col. 3:12–15) Heb. 6:12—Greek *makrothumia,* same for James 5:10, 7–9; 1 Thess. 5:14; 1 Peter 4:14–19.

122. (Gal. 6:9–10; Eph. 6:9; Col. 3:23–4:1; James 2:1–26)

125. (Rom. 12:10–16; James 1:3–5, 12–17; 2 Tim. 2:12; Col. 1:11)

129. Previous Scriptures under 108 (2 Peter 1:3–11; James 3:1–18)

132. Rom. 14:3, 10; 1 Cor. 16:11—Greek *exoutheno:* regard as nothing. 1 Tim. 4:12; 6:2—Greek *kataphroneo:* to think down upon someone.

Appendix E

Factors in Considering the Morality of Birth Control

I. Factors in terms of relationship
  A. Sex is the capstone of the intimate relation of husband and wife
  B. Its importance is upheld in Scripture (1 Cor. 7:2–5)
II. Factors in terms of physiology
  A. The fact that pregnancy can occur only a few days out of each month
  B. The fact that a woman is a woman even without a reproductive system (this companionship relationship continues without the ability or responsibility of reproduction)
  C. Spacing of children not possible without birth control
III. Factors in terms of responsibility
  A. The responsibility to use the knowledge that we have intelligently:
    The more we know, the more God wants us to act responsibly
  B. Responsibility to care for and provide for an inordinate number of children can be stumbling block to total relationship
  C. The responsibility to provide effectively in one's cultural context for children brought into the family
  D. Health of wife and mother to be considered in some cases
  E. Possibility of God's sovereign overruling of birth control efforts

Select Bibliography

Chapman, Gary. *Toward a Growing Marriage.* Chicago, Ill.: Moody Press, 1979.

Fryling, Robert, and Janice Fryling. *A Handbook for Married Couples.* Downers Grove, Ill.: InterVarsity Press, 1984.

Harley, Willard F. *His Needs, Her Needs.* Old Tappan, N. J.: Fleming H. Revell, 1986.

Mack, Wayne, and Nathan Mack. *Preparing for Marriage God's Way.* Tulsa, Okla.: Virgil W. Hensely, Inc., n.d.

Mason, Mike. *The Mystery of Marriage.* Portland, Oreg.: Multnomah Press, 1985.

Rankin, Peg, and Lee Rankin. *Your Marriage: Making It Work.* Batavia, Ill.: Lion Publishing, 1986.

Smalley, Gary, and Steve Scott. *If Only He Knew.* Grand Rapids: Zondervan, 1982.

___. *The Joy of Committed Love.* Grand Rapids: Zondervan, 1988.

Smalley, Gary, and John Trent. *Love Is a Decision.* Waco, Tex.: Word Books, 1989.

___. *The Two Sides of Love.* Pomona, Calif.: Focus on the Family, 1990. Stuart, Richard B. *Couple's Precounseling Inventory.* Champaign, Ill.: Research Press, 1983.

Swihart, Judson J. *How Do You Say "I Love You"?* Downers Grove, Ill.: InterVarsity Press, 1981.

Yorkey, Mike, ed. *Growing a Healthy Home.* Bentwood, Tenn.: Wolgemuth & Hyatt, 1990.

Notes

Introduction

1. Tim and Beverly LaHaye, *The Act of Marriage* (Grand Rapids: Zondervan Publishing House, 1976), p. 13.

2. Richard Chenevix Trench, *Synonyms of the New Testament* (Grand Rapids: William B. Eerdmans Publishing Co., 1963), p. 85.

Chapter 1

1. In conjunction with my doctoral studies, I conducted a research project in premarital counseling. Three approaches to premarital counseling were developed, and engaged couples were enlisted to go through each of the modules. This research was known as the Field Project. From time to time I will refer to this research.

2. This is a simple technique. The pastor appoints the man as responsible for calling the conference at the agreed place and time. He outlines for them guidelines which can help them discuss the problem without arguing and getting bogged down. And he elicits a commitment to function according to these guidelines. I am indebted to Dr. Jay Adams for the outline of this technique, which I observed in counselor training.

3. Pastors should be about the business of educating congregations concerning the need for and practice of premarital counseling. Preaching "plugs" and bulletin notices can serve as reminders.

4. See note 17 under chapter 5.

Chapter 2

1. Jay E. Adams, *The Christian Counselor's Manual* (Nutley, N.J.: Presbyterian and Reformed Publishing Co., 1973). This volume is especially helpful with specific problems. If the reader lacks confidence in this area, I suggest he read *Basic Principles of Biblical Counseling*, by Lawrence J. Crabb, Jr. (Grand Rapids: Zondervan Publishing House, 1975).

2. I have tried to limit the number of volumes included. In my judgment, I have selected the best of the available materials and the best within these materials.

3. Jay E. Adams, *Shepherding God's Flock* (Nutley, N.J.: Presbyterian and Reformed Publishing Co., 1975), vol. II, p. 86.

4. The exception would be if one should become rebellious and refuse to come to the session. The other prospective partner should continue in counseling. This counseling would take the form of remedial work and cease to be premarital in terms of this program.

5. Oneness of financial means is part of the "one flesh" concept of marriage. A division of finances will breed other divisions.

6. This idea first came to my attention through the practice of the Rev. John MacArthur at Grace Community Church in California.

Chapter 4

1. Dr. Eyrich has developed this theme in the foregoing chapters. I will not reiterate it here.

2. Dr. Eyrich has developed such a responsive reading which you will find in Illustration 1. He and I have both experienced positive responses, from wedding families and participating congregations, to this reading.

3. This responsive reading was crafted for my daughter's wedding.

Chapter 5

1. Expressed by Dr. Howard Hendricks in a classroom lecture at Dallas Theological Seminary, 1967.

2. Adams, *The Christian Counselor's Manual,* p. 28.

3. A pastor is wise to discuss his policies regarding weddings when interviewing with the official board of a prospective church. An official notation of the board's acceptance of such policies in the minutes of the proceedings may prevent difficulties at a later date. A current pastor should prepare his policies and his biblical logic for them and present them to his board, seeking to gain their acceptance as official church policy (or at least their official backing).

4. Compare 1 Corinthians 7:39 and 2 Corinthians 6:16ff. Also, see the illustration of Ezra 10.

5. This in no way suggests that a Christian couple might be incompatible and therefore should divorce. Once two believers are married, they are under obligation through the resources of the Holy Spirit and the Word of God to overcome their problems and make the marriage work.

6. Every attempt should be made to evangelize the unbeliever. See part 2, chapter 2, for discussion of this vital opportunity.

7. I know of one marriage which ended in divorce after seventeen years. The wife, just two days prior to the wedding, discovered her fiance's diary. As she leafed through it, she found a detailed account of a sexual exploit. With grave question she went on with the wedding. However, she harbored a resentment and bitterness toward him which spawned ever-entangling difficulties and eventually the divorce. This question may be the means to insuring that such a problem does not develop among those to whom you minister.

8. Adams, *Shepherding God's Flock,* II, 82–83.

9. Dwight Hervey Small, *The Right to Remarry* (Old Tappan, N.J.: Fleming H. Revell Co., 1975), is a plea for reconsideration of this problem. Guy Duty's

Divorce and Remarriage and John Murray's *Divorce* are volumes that every pastor should read.

10. Psychological Publications, Inc., 5300 Hollywood Boulevard, Los Angeles, Calif. 90027. A sample packet is available upon request.

11. It is interesting that 100 percent of the Christians participating in the Field Project reported that they believed the projections of the test were either a "true representation" or "a fairly accurate representation" of themselves.

12. Promotional literature of Psychological Publications, Inc., 5300 Hollywood Boulevard, Los Angeles, Calif. 90027.

13. Psychological Publications, Inc., *Taylor-Johnson Temperament Analysis Manual*, p. 1.

14. Promotional literature of Psychological Publications, Inc.

15. Ibid.

16. "If the T-JTA is repeated at intervals during the counseling or therapy, the profile may give a visual indication of improvement or lack of it." *Taylor-Johnson Temperament Analysis Manual*, p. 9.

17. The Sex Awareness Inventory, developed by the author, is available through the author.

18. A term coined by Jay Adams to refer to facial expressions, tone of voice, eye inflections, and other means of communication often referred to as "body language."

19. See Appendix C for a list of Scriptures which can be used in conjunction with each of the questions on the T-JTA.

20. It is a good practice for the counselor to write out the assignments for the couple. He will advance the pace of the program if each assignment is carefully explained. Encouraging counselees to call during the week for clarification rather than returning to the next session with an unfinished task is also wise.

21. The Marriage Attitude Indicator was developed by the author. It is available through the author.

22. This response form is a modification of one developed by the Rev. John MacArthur of Grace Community Church in California. Exhibits of homework facsimiles will appear at the end of each chapter.

23. Every pastor will want to develop some variation of the program suggested here. Whatever it is, it should be specific, practical, and develop regularity.

Chapter 6

1. See Appendix "D" for biblical references which this author has found of value in conjunction with each question on the test.

2. Revised and expanded: used by permission of James R. Hine, *Your Marriage Analysis and Renewal* (Danville, Ill.: Interstate Publisher and Printer).

3. E. E. LeMasters, *Modern Courtship and Marriage* (New York: Macmillan, 1957), pp. 195–196.

4. Tom McGinnis, *Your First Year of Marriage* (Garden City: Doubleday & Co., Inc., 1967), p. 53.

5. Max and Vivian Rice, *When Can I Say I Love You* (Chicago: Moody Press, 1977). This work has an excellent discussion of this passage. See pp. 17–33.

Chapter 7

1. McGinnis, p. 3.

2. The counselor can better equip himself for this discussion by reading Dwight Hervey Small's *After You've Said I Do* (Old Tappan, N.J.: Fleming H. Revell

Co., 1968) and Jay E. Adams' *Christian Living in the Home* (Nutley, N.J.: Presbyterian and Reformed Publishing Co., 1972), pp.25–42.

3. Dr. John Bettler, addressing the Spring 1976 Eastern Pennsylvania Regional of the Independent Fundamental Churches of America.

4. Compare Matthew 5:21–24 and 18:15–18.

5. Recommended reading on communication: McGinnis, *Your First Year of Marriage,* chaps. 3–4; Dwight Hervey Small, *Design for Christian Marriage* (Old Tappan, N.J.: Fleming H. Revell Co., 1974), pp. 38–50; Small, *After You've Said I Do,* pp. 11–44. Another useful tool in dealing with communication is *A Mental Communication Inventory,* by Millord J. Bienvenu, Sr. Available through Family Life Publications, Inc.

6. For a discussion of biblical roles, see Gene Getz, *The Christian Home in a Changing World* (Chicago: Moody Press, 1972), pp. 22–32, and Adams, *Christian Living in the Home,* pp. 69–101.

7. Small, *After You've Said I Do,* p. 19.

8. Getz correctly observes, "How many generations may need to pass before the effects of this sin (improper family example) will no longer be evident? The fact is that three, four, even five generations of children may be affected, and it is conceivable that the descendants of those who denied the faith may never become Christians" (*The Christian Home in a Changing World,* p. 51). But the grace of God can break the cycle at any time. Good premarital counseling can be the channel through which that grace flows.

9. Small, *Design for Christian Marriage,* pp. 85–86. For further reference see Small, *Design for Christian Marriage,* pp. 20–21, 69–90; Sylvanus Duvall, *Before You Marry* (New York: Association Press, 1969), pp. 26–44; Ellen McKay Trimmer, *Building Interpersonal Relationships* (Chicago: Moody Press, 1972), pp. 47–55; Adams, *Christian Living in the Home,* pp. 87–101.

Chapter 8

1. Number one may provide for the contingency. For example, J. C. Penney's credit cards are good at Thrift Drug Stores.

2. One of my students, Dr. Morely, suggested that as she worked through the budget, it made her aware of "the need to teach our children how to sew, garden and be 'handymen.'"

3. See George M. Bowman, *Here's How to Succeed With Your Money* (Chicago: Moody Press, 1960) for development of a similar idea.

4. To begin to teach children these principles, allowances could be given when children turn ten. The prerequisites to get each week's allowance would be turning in to Dad an accounting of last week's expenditures, which must include a contribution to the Lord.

5. *Christian Family Money Management and Financial Planning* (Ivyland, Pa.: Louis Niebauer Co., 1975).

6. See also Floyd Sharp and Al MacDonald, *Handbook for Financial Faithfulness* (Grand Rapids: Zondervan Publishing House, 1974); Lyle B. Gangesi, *Manual for Group Premarital Counseling* (New York: Association Press, 1971), pp. 221–245; Duvall, *Before You Marry,* pp. 81–109; McGinnis, *Your First Year of Marriage,* pp. 90–97. This is a good discussion for the couple to read. A valuable seminar on Christian Financial Planning is offered by the National Institute of Christian Financial Planning, 1435 Highland Avenue, Melbourne, Florida 32935. Some of the best materials which I have found are produced by Christian Financial Concepts, Inc., and authored by Larry Burkett. The following three works are of particular interest: *Your Finances in Changing Times, Christian*

Financial Concepts, and *Family Planning Workbook.* These may be ordered from Christian Financial Concepts, Inc. 4730 Darlene Way, Tucker, Georgia 30084.

7. See Appendix "E" for some principles to use in discussion of birth control and references for further study.

8. Norman Lobsenz, "Ten Questions Couples Ask Marriage Counselors Most," *Reader's Digest* 108, 650 (June, 1976), p. 72.

9. Each counselor should listen to these tapes before utilizing them. To avoid undue temptation, he may choose to postpone this assignment until a week or two before the wedding. He may profitably schedule an appointment within a few weeks after the marriage to provide opportunity for necessary guidance.

10. The book by Tim and Beverly LaHaye, *The Act of Marriage,* can be recommended as an excellent handbook for the bride and groom in the matter of sexual love. Dr. Wheat has also published a companion book to his tapes, entitled *Intended for Pleasure.* Fleming H. Revell is the publisher. Since the original publication of this book, numerous works on sexual love have been published. The counselor is urged to seek out and review these volumes.

Chapter 9

1. David R. Mace, *Getting Ready for Marriage* (New York: Abingdon Press, 1972), pp. 78–82, would make a good reading assignment for the couple. See also McGinnis, *Your First Year of Marriage,* pp. 85–122.

2. Adams, *The Christian Counselor's Manual,* p. 392. See also LaHaye, *The Act of Marriage,* pp. 11–20. *The Scriptures, Sex and Satisfaction,* by Harry H. McGee, M.D. (Nutley, N.J.: Presbyterian and Reformed Publishing Co., 1975), is a booklet which includes the reproduction of the seven principles compiled by Adams. It could be given to couples as a counseling aid.

3. LaHaye has some interesting helpful discussion in his chapter titled, "Practical Answers to Common Questions," which related to this principle, pp. 234–291.

4. Herbert J. Miles, *Sexual Happiness in Marriage* (Grand Rapids: Zondervan Publishing House, 1967), pp. 76–77, discusses these positions.

5. See McGinnis, pp. 129–138, for fuller discussion. See also the *Journal of Pastoral Practice* I, 2, p. 49. A yearly journal, *Contraceptive Technology,* published under the auspices of the Family Planning division of Emory University Hospital, is available from Halsted Press, a division of John Wiley, 605 Third Avenue, New York, N.Y. This work can keep the pastor-counselor informed of recent developments.

6. Mace, p. 85. See also McGinnis, pp. 143–154, for a good discussion of the in-law problem.

7. Mace, p. 88.

8. Howard Hendricks, *Christian Marriage,* Art of Family Living, P. O. Box 2000, Dallas, Tex. 75221.

9. For further reference see Llewellyn Miller, *The Encyclopedia of Etiquette* (New York: Crown Publishers, Inc., 1967), pp. 512–588. This work provides a complete reference not only for the duties of the wedding party but also for the planning of the entire wedding.

Chapter 10

1. Franklin M. Segler, *The Broadman Minister's Manual* (Nashville: Broadman Press, 1968), p. 30.

2. A list of musical selections appropriate for weddings appears on pp. 145–146.

3. It is wise for the pastor to petition the official board of his church to formulate a written, specific policy on these matters. This can be printed and handed to each couple. Such standardization can prevent inequities or accusations of inequities. Fees for nonmembers can be established at a higher rate. Members' fees should be the minimum that will cover expenses.

4. This list was compiled by Mrs. Patricia Didden and is used by permission.

Chapter 12

1. The love bank is an analogical way of thinking about the feeling aspect of a relationship [see Willard F. Harley, *His Needs, Her Needs* (Old Tappan, NJ: Revell, 1986), p. 27.] The idea is that as one does things which please the other, he or she is making deposits in a mate's love bank. Thus, two things happen. Good feelings are generated and a reserve is established so that when one does something to hurt or disappoint the other by making a withdrawal—a spouse does not automatically lose all feeling for a partner.

2. Charles Sell, *Unfinished Business* (Portland, OR: Multnomah Press, 1989) pp. 34–35.

Chapter 13

1. Jay E. Adams, "Group Therapy," *Lectures in Counseling* (Grand Rapids: Zondervan, 1987). I fully concur with mentor Adams. The material in this chapter is an attempt to structure biblical guidelines to capitalize on our God-given social natures. There is no doubt in my mind that this chapter will generate some criticism (even from my friends). However, I hope it will be realized that I have attempted to add some more "planks" to the super structure (an earlier image applied by Adams to his work) of biblical counseling.

2. See Matthew 19:16–20, 20:19–28.

3. Howard Snyder, *The Problem of Wine Skins* (Downers Grove: InterVarsity Press, 1975).

4. Ron Nicholas, et. al., *Small Group Leaders' Handbook* (Downers Grove, IL: InterVarsity, 1982). Two other books more academic in nature may be of interest. They are: Corey, Gerald and Marianne Schneider Brooks. *Groups: Process and Practice* (Pacific Grove, CA: Cole Publishing Co., 1987) and Dibbert, Michael T. and Frank B. Wichern, *Growth Groups* (Grand Rapids, MI: Ministry Resource Library, Zondervan, 1985).

5. The idea of four stages of group development was proposed by Bob McCoy in an unpublished paper titled, "Stages of Small Groups." This paper may be secured from InterVarsity Christian Fellowship. I am indebted to Judy Johnson for the reference to this paper in the chapter "Stages of Small Groups" in Nicholas, et. al., *Small Group Leaders' Handbook.* I have developed the terms *disorganization, organization, organism* and *deorganization* because they are descriptive of the way the class/group functions.

Master Forms
for Reproduction

A set of laser-produced masters of the forms from *Three to Get Ready,* plus additional materials to enhance your premarital preparation program, are available from the author. Included with the more than fifty pages of material is a permission letter which allows you to reproduce these master forms for your ministry use. The entire set of Premarital Counseling Master Forms can be ordered from:

Dr. Howard Eyrich
Growth Advantage
1203 Saddlemaker Drive
St. Charles, MO 63304